REAKTION BOOKS

For James Helgeson

Published by Reaktion Books Ltd
Unit 32, Waterside
44–48 Wharf Road
London N1 7UX, UK
www.reaktionbooks.co.uk

First published 2017

Printed and bound in China by 1010 Printing International Ltd

A catalogue record for this book is available from the British Library
ISBN 978 1 78023 719 0

OPENING IMAGES: p. 6: A beer garden on the Spree; p. 7: The Quadriga, on the Brandenburg Gate, is the iconic 1793 creation of Johann Gottfried Schadow. Originally a symbol of peace, over time the statue also became a military symbol. Its changing meanings reflect both hopes and fears about Germany's place in European life; p. 8: Kaiser Wilhelm Memorial Church, Breitscheidplatz, and the modern belfry built in 1963; p. 9 (top): Summer in Kreuzberg: a festival in a park; p. 9 (bottom): A midsummer sunset in Volkspark, Prenzlauer Berg; p. 10: The Soviet War Memorial in the Tiergarten; p. 11 (top): A Currywurst kiosk; p.11 (bottom): Café 9, Kreuzberg; pp. 12-13: The 1896 Oberbaum Bridge (Oberbaumbrücke) was a border crossing between East and West Berlin. Today Friedrichshain and Kreuzberg are connected here by the U-Bahn and the party mile, or Technostrich; p. 14 (top): The Berlin Wall (rear side of the East Side Gallery); p. 14 (bottom): Turkish-German women at a market in Mitte; p. 15 (top): Prenzlauer Berg; p. 15 (bottom): Outside the KitKatClub in Mitte. The poster reads: 'Here Berlin club culture has existed for decades. We ask for thoughtfulness in your apartment-building projects.'

Contents

ВЕЧНАЯ СЛАВА
ГЕРОЯМ ПАВШИМ
В БОЯХ С НЕМЕЦКО
ФАШИСТСКИМИ
ЗАХВАТЧИКАМИ
ЗА СВОБОДУ И
НЕЗАВИСИМОСТЬ
СОВЕТСКОГО
СОЮЗА
1941
1945

CURRY
Am Ku'damm
COLD DRINKS
COLD DRINKS

Hier exist
seit Jahrzehnten
Berliner Clubkultur!
Wir bitten um
ücksicht bei Ihrem
entumswohnungs-
Bauvorhaben.
SAGE CLUB

Remains of the Berlin Wall along Bernauer Strasse, between the districts of Mitte and Wedding.

Prologue

Berlin has an inimitable aesthetic. On arriving, from the taxi window, one is struck by the detritus of the twentieth century: derelict warehouses, the glint of the sprawling railway tracks, buildings orphaned next to lots once devastated by war damage. In the background are rows of Communist-era block housing. A disused factory might have a new purpose: a swimming pool turned arts space, or power plant turned nightclub. Peeling walls are mottled with decades of street art; they reveal the buildings' former lives, their past degradations. That newly whitewashed surface, in the foreground, will not last long before it is attacked. You accelerate along the leafy canals, where grass grows wild, untended; the city's cost-cutting dovetails with a fondness for the unkempt. The absence of a foursquare grid plan allows a disorderly asymmetry. It is a haphazard cityscape – *Blade Runner* meets the urban pastoral – that pulses with potential. Berlin invites an aestheticizing of the decrepit, the shattered, the imperfect, the dissonant. You are asked to cast your imagination into the industrial ruins. It is a little like being solicited to listen to Alban Berg – or, for that matter, minimal electronica – after an afternoon of Gaetano Donizetti on the radio. After a few weeks here, you might never be satisfied with a freshly painted wall again.

Perhaps there are moral qualities to this Berlin aesthetic. It privileges process and time passing; it is a reminder that nothing is fixed. The Neues Museum is an illuminating example: here the bombing damage is not patched up but exposed, recalling how war brutalized Berlin, as Berlin brutalized Europe. The weight of past crimes, the fact that the city has been a laboratory of ideologies and the command centre for their victims, is inescapable. With this comes a heightened historical mindfulness, with the many memorials and a strong public culture of remembrance. Perhaps that's why walls are not whitewashed, but allowed to peel.

The omnipresent graffiti, the general deficiency of mass advertising and the fact that so much space in Berlin continues to be undeveloped despite recent gentrification gives Berlin an anti-authoritarian and not entirely streamlined feel. For a long time half-Communist, the capital is an affront to the mass-produced, consumerist, capitalistic mode of standardized living that dominates most Western cities.

Nor is there a standard Berliner. The moment your train pulls into the busy interchange of Alexanderplatz, the crowd piles in and you are faced with a barrage of tattoos, unusual haircuts, Taliban-hipster facial hair and sharp-edged German eyewear. The fashionable mix with those in workaday proletarian garb. Two journeymen apprentices in medieval overalls stand above the camera-laden tourists. An Italian couple looks out of place – Berlin is decidedly a city that dresses down – in their Versace holiday wear. The flowing veils of Turkish women pushing strollers billow around the embassy flunky carrying a briefcase. Swarming the doors are a group of party kids, flushed and half-clothed, carrying open containers, fresh from the Technostrich (the clubbers' catwalk over the Oberbaumbrücke – they got on the S-Bahn at Warschauer Strasse). Your morning is only their late evening. They could have walked out of a Wolfgang Tillmans photograph. There is the smell of sex somewhere. One has his hand down his boyfriend's trousers. No one deigns to notice – it's Berlin, after all.

Maybe the lack of propriety is because the petit bourgeois, or *spiessig*, is oppressed here. The base culture of Berlin is proletarian, and many Berliners are suspicious of national codes. Parts of the city are full of immigrants from Turkey, Lebanon and elsewhere, mixing with a recent influx of internationals and refugees. All this means that expectations to acculturate are diminished.

Young people from all over Europe are moving to Berlin not simply because of the (still) low cost of living, in a continent that seems to have fewer and fewer possibilities. They are perhaps drawn to that strange land lurking outside the city limits, called Germany, which provides its poorish capital – at least for now – with a functioning social system, growth and stability. For artists, there is the concentration of camaraderie and opportunity. The city overflows with music and theatre events, and not just in its better-known cultural institutions. This creative buzz of exchange means it is remarkably easy to meet people. Perhaps too easy. One's life becomes a vortex of metropolitan vanities, the kind of *mondain* flutter that gives a city its moment, according to the press – Paris in the 1920s, New York in the 1950s and undoubtedly Berlin today.

New Berliners, and especially young tourists, are drawn by Europe's party capital – and you never know what is going to happen to you when you walk out of that door. The scene is exciting enough to get many Italians and Spaniards to trade the Mediterranean sun for dark winter nights; it's a worthwhile exchange if it means escaping the prudishness of their families and the economic crisis as well. Their arrival is having a palpable effect on the volume of conversation in Berlin's many bars, as they are joined by Brits, Americans, Chinese, Japanese, Brazilians and others looking for more intangible attractions. Because this city feels unfinished, there is room for experimentation, opportunities to 'remake' yourself.

All this might take some getting used to. Those expecting the standardized oppression of statuesque Europe – manicured lawns, Baroque fountains, symmetrical city squares with uninterrupted ancient facades and ornate palaces – are not going to find themselves in an archetypal Continental city. It is not that the Old World does not exist here – the city is full of cultivated lakeside walks and restaurants with white tablecloths – it's just not what distinguishes Berlin. Perhaps Berlin's charm is that you can go from the Baroque Charlottenburg Palace to the industrial stretch of Friedrichshain in less than half an hour.

That said, the former mayor's quip that 'Berlin is poor, but sexy' has been repeated excessively, and one might wonder whether it is still accurate. Is Berlin so exceptional? The Berlin aesthetic has been something of an inspiration, or a stereotype, for other cities, and has melded into a more generalized hipster aesthetic, cross-pollinated between Berlin, Detroit, east London and Brooklyn, and now found worldwide. Money has meanwhile been flowing into the city, partly because Berlin has been discovered by tourists, making it the third most popular traveller destination in Europe. It's now possible that that funky bar with the Berlin aesthetic simply hired a group of young people to graffiti its bathrooms one afternoon, to make it look like a 1990s original. That new Michelin-rated restaurant, or the local branch of the Soho Club, with exposed concrete and peeling walls, wants to remind you, too, that you are 'in Berlin'. Meanwhile, a wealthy expat living in a building with a scruffy entrance, which mandatorily eschews any sign of pomp and remains 'down to earth', owns a ridiculously stylish loft on the top floor. Gentrification, rising rent prices and the paradoxical standardization of a non-standardized aesthetic make some wonder whether Berlin is 'over'. Perhaps this is so if one measures Berlin by 'superclubs' like Berghain, located in a former GDR power plant, which have long been discovered by the Easyjetset. But the city is so vast that the alternative nightspots have simply moved farther out from the centre. Those old-timers still looking for edge in Mitte had better get themselves a transit pass. Some say: you can still have a wild time in Berlin, but at least now it's also possible to have a good meal. The 'Berlin Renaissance', as it is called, is not over, but perhaps it is entering its decadent phase.

Taking a more local perspective, rather than measuring the city by its party scene – a strange metric if there ever was one – the socially conscious are focusing on widening economic disparities. Investors and the moneyed international set, often English-speaking (there is an overlap), in creative industries or start-ups, live rather differently from the still comparatively poor 'Berliner' population, joined by large numbers of asylum seekers. This discrepancy gives Berlin an increasingly 'town and gown' feel. Meanwhile, on the geopolitical stage, others fear that the problem is not that Berlin is 'over' – if only! Berlin's star is finally rising again, as the resurgent capital of Europe's most troublesome power, armed with austerity policies rather than Panzers.

Berlin might not always be beautiful, but it is intriguing. This book intends to introduce this remarkable capital, first through its history, and then by visiting the city today. The latter section's 'today' is Berlin in the first months of 2017; how I see it now. This portrait will change (and fundamentally, because Berlin remains a construction site) and become a document of a moment in time. That said, I do think it will be a while before 'The City Today' is relegated to the first section of this book, 'History'.

As you explore, you might find that those elements of Berlin that are unnerving – its emptiness, its green sniff of provincialism, its ramshackle industrial eclecticism, its sexual freedoms, its confrontation with a murderous past – are precisely what, for a certain kind of personality, give the city its charge. Berlin will remain, one hopes, a place that bucks stereotypes and challenges the expectations of an Epcot Europe. It remains a capital that has something more to offer than narrow national prescriptions for how to dress, eat or act *en ville*.

Instead, you get smoke, sweat, sex and blunt conversation, all rolled up in a reflective, guilty conscience. Is it Europe's creative heart or its black hole and dropout capital? The escape hatch from the market, or the quiet at the centre of capitalism's storm? The decadent eye of a Europe in decline? I'm not sure, but its gravity is palpable, dark and exciting – and it's hard not to feel its tug.

On top of the 1864 Victory Column (*Siegessäule*) is Friedrich Drake's statue of Victoria. The Berliners call her *Goldelse*, or Gold Liza. The column was widened in 1939 to compensate for her large size.

HISTORY

1 Before Prussia (until 1701)

When the ice receded, it left a shallow glacial valley strung with lakes and bogs, with peat and mud deposits. The higher ground was a mix of clay with lime. Almost everything else was sand. It is the same sand driven later by wind down the streets, covering piles of rubble after the Second World War. Or that today is the bane of construction crews still rebuilding a city reduced to the ground. More than a third of all trees lining today's city streets are lindens, which can grow in sand and loam. Turn on your tap in Berlin and the water is unusually hard, having filtered through the lime. Even the ancient name of Berlin comes from this shifting landscape: the Slavic *Brlo* means a dry place in a bog.

This etymology hints at yet another aspect of Berlin's origins, the fact that 'Germans' did not arrive here in numbers, to displace the Slavic 'Wends', until the rule of Albrecht the Bear, who invaded from Saxony (the Slavic world is still not far away, with the Polish border today only 50 km as the crow flies). 'The Bear' declared himself the Margrave of the Mark Brandenburg, the region surrounding Berlin, in the middle of the twelfth century. The phonetic, though not etymological, association of 'Berlin' with *Bär* (or bear) might be the reason the city adopted the animal as its heraldic beast by the fifteenth century.

Brandenburg is a basin, recognizable as soon as you pass into it by train from the south, carved out by the ice sheet, and distinguished from the more temperate Central Europe by its relentless flatness. But it also has softness, from what appear like endless forests, curving around the lakes. They make Berlin seem stuck in some verdant biosphere in midsummer when one peers from any gentle rise over the otherwise sheer landscape. Today, at the entrance of the exhibits of the German Historical Museum, there is a large-scale photograph of these woods. If you stand at an angle the 'Germans' appear superimposed in hologram, clothed in medieval garb: braided cloaks, woollen tunics, linen shirts or women's long shifts. These people – defined more by their landscape, local culture and family connections than by anything they would recognize as 'Germanness' – established settlements at that dry place in the marsh, and built a bridge where the Spree river narrows ever so slightly.

Two market towns, called Berlin and Cölln, eventually faced one another, the latter located on an island in the river, now the Museum Island. But how early is a matter of debate – neither one of these small communities was significant enough to be dated by city charter. And the first times Berlin and Cölln are mentioned in writing, in 1244 and 1237 respectively, they appear in tax and administrative documents referring to the same person, which makes one wonder how distinct the two entities were in the early thirteenth century. Cölln so lacked its own civic identity that it took its name from somewhere else, Rheinlanders perhaps having named it after the great city with Roman origins in the West. And we know Berlin was tiny compared to nearby settlements, like Spandau, now just a Berlin suburb. When looking at the twelfth-century model in the Märkisches Museum, one sees that Spandau was just rows of rudimentary shacks surrounded by a timber wall. But the insignificance of Berlin-Cölln has not prevented civil authorities, as a matter of pride, from celebrating an exact founding date. The discovery of an oak plank from 1183 was heralded by the City of Berlin in 2008 as the first indication of settlement, making Berlin 54 years older than previously thought.

It was only in the late thirteenth century that Berlin-Cölln grew in wealth and numbers. It did so by taking advantage of its location. The two market posts flourished in the trade of fish and textiles from Flanders. By damming the Spree, the clever early Berliners forced traders to stop and sell their wares

St Nicholas Church (Nikolaikirche), 13th century.

in the city. The crossing of Mühlendamm between Berlin and Cölln was so named because it was the location of water-powered grain mills. Focusing on these waterways, however, is only part of the story, as Berlin was also an important highway junction on both the east–west and north–south axes. Growing wealth brought with it the need for civil administration, and two councils were established that cooperated, facing each other across the long bridge. Today's City Hall is situated at the same location as Berlin's first authority. Many historians emphasize the fact that Berlin started as a divided city, but here we get ahead of ourselves. These towns were of course not under separate ideological systems, as Berlin would be in the mid-twentieth century. Cölln eventually joined Berlin administratively in 1307, in a town now of several thousand surrounded by a wall and gates. The *Stadtmauer*, or city wall of Berlin, endured in different versions, and increasing heights, in circumference around Berlin and Cölln island until the building of the much bigger Customs Wall in 1734. Remains of the early wall can be seen on Littenstrasse, not far from Alexanderplatz. Nearby are the medieval Nikolaikirche, where a Romanesque stone church once stood in the thirteenth century, and the ruins of a Franciscan monastery from around 1250 at Grunerstrasse.

From a beginning when we have a mercantile people profiting mostly off the goods that pass through a harsh landscape – rather than trying to soak their living out of the poor sandy soil – we now shift into a period of expansion. It would take the Hohenzollern family to shape this space and make it imperial in character. How striking that this dry place in a mucky mix of water and loose banks would become the capital of Europe's largest and most troublesome power, a city at times feared and despised. Perhaps it is worth reflecting that only such a poor upstart of a city, this latecomer capital on a swampy plain, without natural boundaries in any direction, would need to remain so much on the offence.

It is remarkable that one royal house, the Hohenzollern, ruled Berlin for more than half a millennium, from the fifteenth to the twentieth century. But they were originally considered parvenu conquerors who had come to the city from the south and acquired Brandenburg only because the House of Luxembourg had defaulted on its debts. Their

Remains of the medieval city wall on Littenstrasse.

family castle at Zollern was *hohe*, or 'high', because it was located in the Swabian Alps, a landscape alien to the flatlands of the north. Their desire to build a palace in Berlin was not welcomed by the locals, who were unwilling to cede the power of their councils on the long bridge. Friedrich I (1371–1440) left the job unfinished for his successor, Friedrich II, the Irontoothed (1413–1471), who ran into trouble when the locals vandalized his efforts by flooding the island's building site in 1448. Having already taken Berlin out of the Hanseatic League, he diminished civic power further by having the councils torn down; the piecemeal construction of the palace then continued for almost three hundred years. The struggle of a liberal, mercantile city population at odds with its conservative imperial rulers is a theme that can be charted even into the twentieth century. The later Baroque iteration of the palace – which was finished in 1716, damaged in the Second World War, then razed by the German Democratic Republic (GDR) – is now being rebuilt, much to the ire of many Berliners for whom it represents the ills of Prussian authoritarianism.

By the sixteenth century, Berlin had 10,000 inhabitants, and its ruler Joachim II Hector (1505–1571) was determined

Ruins of the 13th-century Franciscan cloister, Grunerstrasse.

The Baroque *Zeughaus* (Arsenal) of 1695, home of the German Historical Museum.

to increase his royal trappings: a hunting palace in Grunewald, to the west, connected to the area around Berlin by a wooded avenue (the Kurfürstendamm, which is now Berlin's most luxurious street). Too much time spent outside Berlin – at Grunewald and elsewhere – hunting instead of governing had unexpected consequences for the Elector. The floor of the country retreat of Grimnitz gave way one evening under him and his wife. She was impaled on the antlers of his hunting trophies below as he hung precariously from the beams. Although she survived the fall, her deformity gave him the excuse to set up with his mistress.

Although Joachim II had promised his father to remain Catholic, he received Communion according to the Lutheran rite on 1 November 1539. Town and crown, however, would soon be further divided. Elector John Sigismund (1572–1619) converted to Calvinism, even though the majority of his subjects remained Lutheran.

Friedrich Wilhelm (1620–1688) consolidated Calvinist rule. It was the Thirty Years War (1618–1648), fought initially between the Protestant and Catholic kingdoms of Europe

and resolved by the Treaty of Westphalia, which would have a defining influence on his reign. Brandenburg had been a battleground, and marauding soldiers still terrorized its lands. The young man of 23 returned to Berlin in 1643 to see his city in ruins. The population had been halved by war and plague, leaving it in a 'zero hour' (Berlin would have another). The devastation had a lasting impression on him, and he was determined to rebuild, keep the country on the offensive and raise a professional army. His rule saw an expansion of territories: the landlocked Mark Brandenburg, and islands of dependence to the west, absorbed a huge swathe of contiguous sea-coast in Pomerania in 1648, to add to the eastern Baltic Duchy of Prussia, which had been inherited by the Hohenzollerns in 1618. He earned the title 'Great Elector' through a series of military victories towards the end of the seventeenth century: at the Battle of Warsaw in 1656, and when routing the Swedes' so-called invincible army at Brandenburg in 1675. By the end of his rule, his lands had a standing army of 20,000. With the Great Elector, one can see the foundations of the Prussian military state. Having experienced the trauma of being Europe's battlefield for thirty

Early 20th-century view of what was Cölln.

years, Prussia would counter its vulnerability by investing heavily in armed protection.

In Berlin, Friedrich Wilhelm's urban renewal progressed with the building of a long avenue planted with lime trees and called Unter den Linden, leading from the royal palace to the location of what would be the Brandenburg Gate. Improvements in public infrastructure included building primitive sewers, cobbling streets, installing street lights and banishing barns outside the walls, as a fire risk, to the *Scheunenviertel*, or 'Barn District'. Having studied among his co-religionists in Utrecht, the Netherlands (a land, of course, that was influential in the seventeenth century), he took from there some ideas for how to manage the problem of Brandenburg's bogs and flooding by copying the canal system, building a series of waterways crossed by Dutch drawbridges between 1669 and 1671.

The Great Elector's allegiance to Calvinism, however, is best observed in his response to a wave of émigré French Protestants. In 1685, the Edict of Nantes, which had resolved the Wars of Religion in France in 1598, was revoked. The Great

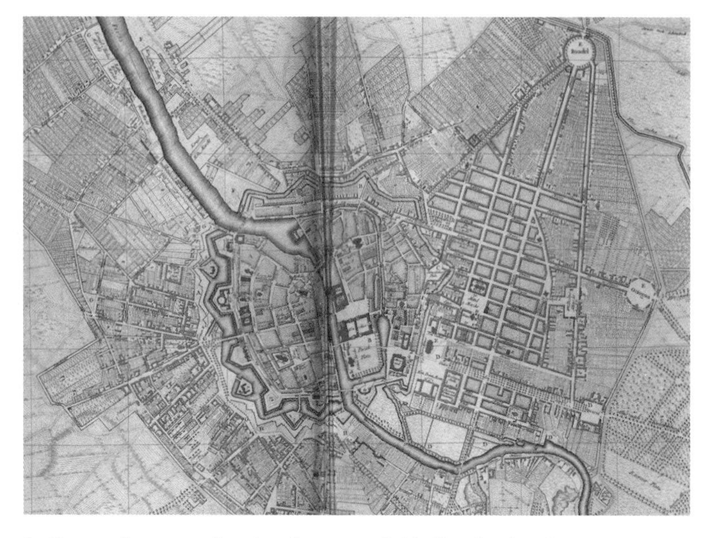

Berlin map from 1757, showing the centre divided by the river Spree.

Elector, in solidarity with his Calvinist co-religionists, eager to repopulate Brandenburg-Prussia after the wars, proclaimed the Edict of Potsdam, or of Tolerance, the same year. It allowed freedom of religious practice (Catholics, mind you, were not invited) and gave immigrants tax-free status for a decade. Twenty thousand of them would find their way to Brandenburg, meaning that almost a quarter of the population of the city was French-speaking by 1700. In the same spirit, Berlin would later host, in the eighteenth century, thousands of Bohemian Protestants who were followers of Jan Hus in exile.

The other major group that arrived as part of Berlin's 'imported bourgeoisie' were the Jews. There had been flickers of Jewish life in Berlin before the seventeenth century: they had been subject to pogroms, one in response to a breakout of haemorrhagic fever in 1356, another when 38 Jews were hanged on the city gates in 1510 for allegedly desecrating the Host. The most significant event, however, was the arrival in 1671 of fifty Jewish families who had been expelled from Vienna. They were welcomed because they brought with them capital and paid for their right of residence. While the French were given tax-free benefits and special assistance in

Museum Island as it appears in an album from 1903.

the organization of their visas and arrival in Berlin, and built a great church of thanks to the Germans in 1701 (the Germans built their response, a 'German' church, across the famous Gendarmenmarkt in the same period), the Jewish population, one thousand in number by 1701, was forbidden from building a public synagogue, subject to a revocable right of residence, a poll and many other forms of tax, and made collectively responsible for criminal acts. It was only forty years after the arrival of the Vienna Jews, in 1712, that a synagogue was finally built in Heidereuterstrasse. Jews were settled after 1737 in precarious conditions adjacent to the Barn District, where property prices far exceeded the quality of housing.

Museum Island, as it appeared during renovations of the Berlin City Palace in 2016.

THE HUGUENOTS AND BERLIN DIALECT

French immigration had a profound effect on the city's culture. It would have a strong impact on the Berlin dialect (now better preserved in the former East than West), with phrases still in use such as *Mir ist janz blümerant* (I've got a queasy feeling, from *bleu mourant*) or *Bring ma nich in de Bredullje* (don't get me into trouble, from *être bredouillé*). If you've been to a beer garden in Berlin you know you don't order a *Fleischkloss*, but a Gallic *Bulette*. Indeed, not only were there new words, but new foods. Some refugees, coming from Provence, would eventually settle in the south of Berlin, in an area that would later be called the Luisenstadt. They excelled in the cultivation of exotic produce such as citrus fruit, green peas and artichokes, not to mention asparagus, which is now a regional speciality. The glasshouses of the Matthieu family, who were the first seed vendors in Germany, lasted until 1853 in the district; some speculate that the legacy of the citrus fruit cultivation in the heart of Kreuzberg is still visible in the street signs: what was called Orangenstrasse in 1709 became Oranienstrasse by 1849, although both are more likely to be associated with the House of Orange. Although Germany's Federal Minister of the Interior under the Merkel government, who has Huguenot roots, is named Thomas de Maizière, French surnames are uncommon today. We have Germany's many conflicts with its great neighbour to thank for making them unpopular.

The French Church (1701, remodelled in 1785) in Gendarmenmarkt, built for the Huguenots, with Berlin's Konzerthaus on the left.

Conditions in Berlin, though terribly unjust, were nonetheless better than elsewhere in Europe. At the turn of the eighteenth century, one can already observe the profoundly multicultural direction of the city and its remarkable ability to absorb peoples, but also the vulnerability of those who arrived, especially the Jews, whose story would be a tragic one.

Less than half a millennium had passed from the first mention of Berlin as an inconspicuous market at a river crossing. By 1701, Berlin had more than 50,000 residents, a city core with differing neighbourhoods and a diverse international population. It was the seat for lands extending from the far east of the Baltic to principalities on the Rhine. It even had two small colonies in West Africa. With the crowning of Friedrich I and the establishment of a kingdom, it became the capital of Prussia, an emerging European power.

2 The Kingdom of Soldiers and Philosophers (1701–1871)

The phrase that Prussia was not a 'state with an army, but an army with a state' is attributed to the French revolutionary drunkard Mirabeau. Travellers to Berlin, like James Boswell in 1764, saw young conscripts who 'for the least fault . . . were beat like dogs'. He continued, 'I am, however, doubtful if such fellows don't make the best soldiers. Machines are surer instruments than men.' Indeed, the Berlin customs wall (*Zoll- und Akzisemauer*) of the Prussian capital – built in the 1730s, made of wood reinforced in places with brick – was constructed not only to repel foreign invaders, and to tax goods and Jews who passed through it, but to prevent men in uniform from escaping their service. And yet, paradoxically, this Prussia was also a bastion of religious tolerance and Enlightenment philosophy. It was the city of the Mendelssohns, Hegel and Schopenhauer. Much later, historians would speculate about the 'Special Path', or *Sonderweg*, of German history. How could a land that sheltered such towering works of philosophy eventually unleash Europe's most lethal armies?

Many deliberate on the first three Prussian Friedrichs of the eighteenth century, whose family history was unusually explosive. We have, popularly imagined: Friedrich III, the pompous but intelligent spendthrift who crowned himself king in Prussia in 1701 (renaming himself Friedrich I, much to the annoyance of students of history); Friedrich Wilhelm I, from 1713, his reactive frugal militarist son, with a brutal authoritarian streak; and then the synthesis, Friedrich the Great, from 1740, a master statesman, as passionate about his own expansionist military programme as he was about playing the flute.

This mosaic, in the remains of the Kaiser Wilhelm Memorial Church (1895), depicts the dynasties of the House of Hohenzollern.

The pomp of Friedrich I's (1657–1713) self-crowning raised some eyebrows in European aristocratic circles. He did not cut a very regal figure, being Shakespearean in appearance, with a twisted spine and hunchback resulting from an accident in his youth – Berliners named him 'crooked Fritz'. He was a man who, like his forefathers, loved palaces, and it was under his rule that the Hohenzollern residence, the City Palace, began to be transformed into the Baroque style. This and other capital projects, such as the Arsenal (*Zeughaus*), were entrusted to the architect Andreas Schlüter. Friedrich I's second wife, Sophia Charlotte (1668–1705), meanwhile cultivated the friendship of the philosopher Gottfried Leibniz, who became the first president of the Prussian Academy of Sciences. A massive palace bearing her name, Charlottenburg, was built outside the city walls.

His son, Friedrich Wilhelm I, the 'Soldier King' (1688–1740), would criticize the first king of Prussia as prodigal. But the younger monarch only cut back on spending elsewhere to invest in the military. One might expect his rule to have featured many military exploits, but in fact he never initiated a conflict and was drawn into just one. Only ever appearing in public in uniform, the Soldier King put a quarter of all of Prussia into uniform, a total of 100,000 soldiers, with 12,000 soldiers stationed in Berlin alone. The needs of the armed forces would create a tradition of engineering and textile production, making arms and uniforms, which would last into the twentieth century. With these changes, the surface area of Berlin doubled and the population grew to almost 100,000 people.

The tendency of soldiers to want to escape the hardships of Prussian military life led to the construction of the Customs Wall. Also added were parade grounds in the geometric forms of a *Quarré*, *Oktogon* and *Rondell* (Pariser Platz, Leipziger Platz and Belle-Alliance-Platz, now Mehringplatz). The Customs Wall stretched along current-day Torstrasse in the north (named for the *Tore* or 'gates' that punctuated the periphery) and Skalitzer Strasse in the south. Gates leading to the southern towns and regions – the gates of Halle (Hallesches Tor), Cottbus (Kottbusser Tor) and Silesia (Schlesisches Tor) – are now the names of U1-Bahn stations that run along the length of the space left by the former wall.

The Charlottenburg Palace, in a print from the late 19th century.

The most famous gate to the west would be the Brandenburg Gate, the symbol of the city, associated with the reunification of Germany. The gate, designed by Carl Gotthard Langhans under the rule of Friedrich Wilhelm II and completed in 1791, was originally meant to symbolize peace. It was an elegant architectural statement, a model of balance. Its classical proportions and graceful sculptures would later frame, however, a serene goddess leading a horse-drawn quadriga and decorated with the Iron Cross.

But we are anticipating events, and must return to the Soldier King, with whom so much of Prussia's militarism is associated. The relationship between Friedrich Wilhelm I and his son was remarkably tense. The latter, at first, could not shoot well and often fell off his horse. We can imagine the ire of his strict father. But to make matters worse, the son enjoyed poetry and music and spent all his time with a handsome young man suspected of being his lover. It's worth noting that the father's amusements were somewhat different: he and his hard-drinking male advisors famously tortured a courtier, thinking it amusing to lock him in a room with bears while lighting explosives hung from the ceiling. After it was announced that

Forum Fridericianum, the 18th-century architectural showpiece of Friedrich II, picturing the Old Royal Library, now housing the Faculty of Law of Humboldt University.

Before the current Brandenburg Gate was built in 1791, a more modest crossing led to the forests beyond. This drawing, from 1764, is by the Polish-German etcher Daniel Chodowiecki.

he was to be married, young Friedrich attempted to escape; the Soldier King, in one of history's most brutal examples of parental discipline, imprisoned his son in the dungeon of a fortress, and had his possible lover beheaded in front of his cell window. We can only speculate about the psychological effects on the man who would become Prussia's most celebrated monarch.

Under Friedrich II, or 'the Great' (1712–1786), Berlin emerged as a culturally engaged capital following the French Enlightenment model. He redeveloped Unter den Linden with building projects, most notably the Forum Fridericianum. Located on Bebelplatz, it reflected a number of aspects of the monarch: his love of music (the Opera House was the first built independent of a palace north of the Alps), his belief in religious tolerance (St Hedwig's, a Catholic cathedral in a Protestant kingdom) and his passion for reading (the Royal Library). He also built a summer palace at Potsdam called Sanssouci, or 'No Worries'. The Berlin projects in the Palladian style were located not far from the Baroque projects of his grandfather, giving the architecture of Berlin an eclectic feel. Finally, the city could start to compare itself to other European capitals. As Johann Kaspar Riesbeck remarked in 1784: 'Berlin is a remarkably beautiful and magnificent city, and

The Brandenburg Gate, photographed in 1896.

may certainly be looked upon as one of the finest in Europe. It has nothing of the uniformity, which in the long run makes the appearance of most of the new and regular built towns tiresome.' Heterogeneity is still one of the city's defining qualities today.

Court life was permissive. Friedrich the Great famously pardoned a man who had been found penetrating a donkey, with the quip: 'In Prussia, man has freedom of both his head and his "tail" [a synonym for penis in German].' He was an atheist who abolished torture, and the salon life that surrounded him flourished. Voltaire would slander his homosexual tendencies, but Immanuel Kant would celebrate the relative enlightenment of his rule, with the famous aphorism: 'Argue as much as you like, then obey!' Friedrich himself, when questioned by the philosophers of the many salons about those of other faiths, said: 'Even if Turks and heathens came

The Brandenburg Gate as it appears today.

and wanted to populate this country, then we would build mosques and temples for them.' In this respect, he was about 250 years ahead of his time.

The relative openness of Friedrich the Great's Berlin allowed certain Jewish subjects to flourish in both business and the arts. A small number of so-called 'Court Jews' lived in a different universe from poorer Orthodox Jews. The Ephraim family did well from minting currency, for example, and their elegant palace still stands across from the old mint in the heart of Mitte.

A young Moses Mendelssohn (1729–1786) arrived in Berlin from Dessau through the Rosenthaler Gate (now Platz) on the northern boundary of the Customs Wall in 1743. Because he was Jewish, he was taxed, as was livestock. It has been said that the history of literature in Berlin began on that day. Mendelssohn became a role model for Jews who wished to acculturate into German society but keep their religion. He arrived in Berlin speaking only a form of Yiddish, but eventually was able to translate the Torah into High German. For this reason he is known as the father of Reformed Judaism and the leader of the Jewish Enlightenment, or the *Haskalah*.

Mendelssohn provided a test case for the limits of tolerance in Friedrich the Great's Prussia. He famously refused to convert when challenged by a Swiss deacon, although his grandchildren, including the composer Felix Mendelssohn, were eventually baptized. In replying to his Swiss critic, Moses Mendelssohn pointed out,

> Do not the laws of your native city forbid your circumcised friend even to visit you in Zurich? How grateful my coreligionists would be to the dominant nation that includes them in the universal love of mankind and allows them unhindered to pray to the Almighty according to the ways of their fathers! They enjoy a most respectable degree of freedom in the state where I dwell.

Indeed, despite his religion and the social barriers that remained between the Prussian elites and Berlin's wealthy Jewish class, Mendelssohn managed to have a number of famous interreligious friendships within Berlin's flourishing salon scene, most notably with the writer and Enlightenment thinker Gotthold Ephraim Lessing. The Prussian Academy – in the period when Voltaire came to Berlin – elected him a member, but the limits of full acceptance became clear when Friedrich the Great vetoed the move, stating that 'Mendelssohn has everything but a foreskin.' And this from a man who, in his younger years, was noted for the phrase: 'Let every man seek heaven in his own fashion.'

Friedrich the Great's love of the arts, and his relative tolerance of philosophers, however, did not preclude a love of armies – which he used to conquer Silesia and partition Poland while the sound of his flute was heard over the army encampments. It was his success in raising Prussia's military profile that earned him the praise of nineteenth-century nationalists and the Nazis. It also brought him the ire of the disillusioned of the late twentieth century, despite recent efforts to rehabilitate him as a man of culture and tolerance on the 300th anniversary of his birth.

By the end of Friedrich II's rule, the population of Berlin numbered 150,000, about a quarter that of Paris. He was succeeded by Friedrich Wilhelm II (1744–1797), who did his best to restore religious authority and work against the Enlightenment, although he was also known for his interest in mysticism and pleasure seeking. Called *der Vielgeliebte* or 'the much-beloved', the morbidly obese monarch fathered more than half a dozen children, many of whom may have been produced in his pleasure palace or *Lustschloss*. It was built for a mistress in 1797 just within the Berlin city limits, on the Peacock Island, or *Pfaueninsel*, in the Havel river.

His son, the long-ruling Friedrich Wilhelm III (1770–1840), would have the thankless task of leading Prussia through the great period of instability of the first half of the nineteenth century, as Berlin tumbled, with most of Europe, into war with the arrival of French troops in 1806 under Napoleon, who entered Berlin on 27 October. Napoleon was eventually defeated near Leipzig in the Battle of the Nations in October 1813, the largest European battle before the First World War: half a million soldiers were involved.

The Napoleonic Wars brought nationalist and democratic ideas and failed revolutions. Life in Berlin was transformed once more by contact with the French, who this time were conquerors rather than immigrants. Civic power, always subordinated to the needs of the Prussian rulers, reasserted itself with the re-establishment of a town council in 1808 and the demand for voting rights. In this period too, the Friedrich-Wilhelms-Universität was established (1810). Jews benefited from citizenship under the Napoleonic Code, and this would lead in the nineteenth century to even greater advances in Jewish acculturation into Berlin society.

The period of restoration following the French defeat was symbolized by the return in 1814 of the Brandenburg Gate's quadriga from Paris after Napoleon's theft of it; the goddess

Karl Friedrich Schinkel's stage designs for Mozart's *The Magic Flute* (shown here is Karl Friedrich Thiele's copy of the 'Hall of Stars in the Palace of the Queen of the Night', from Act I, Scene 6).

was now militarized, with the Iron Cross in her olive wreath. The Prussian establishment pushed back at the advances of republicanism, and the most important post in Berlin became that of the repressive authority of the Police Superintendent, who imposed the censorship and oppression of the *Vormärz*, or period between 1815 and the failed March 1848 revolutions. Jewish civil equality remained broadly in place in Prussia, although certain rights continued to be curtailed until 1847.

The pedestrian, moralizing, repressed and indecisive Friedrich Wilhelm III nonetheless commissioned some of Berlin's most famous architectural projects. His restoration involved the reinstating of legitimacy through buildings meant to project the permanence of royal power in the Neoclassical style. For this, he turned to the architect Karl Friedrich Schinkel (1781–1841), who between 1816 and 1836 built a number of Berlin's most famous edifices: the Neue Wache guardhouse (1818), the Schauspielhaus (1821) and the Bauakademie (1836, which many call 'proto-modernist'). But perhaps the most beautiful of Schinkel's creations were the 1816 stage designs for a production of Mozart's *The Magic Flute* at the Royal Opera House.

University life in this period also produced some of the most combative minds of the German tradition. Arthur Schopenhauer (1788–1860) arrived in 1811 to study at the University of Berlin with his 'cigars, pistols, flute . . . and very intelligent poodle', and proceeded to fall in and out of love with the teachings of Johann Gottlieb Fichte, whom he at first took for a 'great philosopher and a great mind' but soon came to view with 'disdain and scorn'. By 1820, he was teaching at the university himself and had come to loathe the philosopher G.W.F. Hegel. Calling him a 'clumsy and nauseating charlatan', Schopenhauer famously scheduled his lectures at the same time as his enemy. Perhaps he assumed that students would understand him better than his foe, who had a muddy Swabian accent. Nevertheless, only five students turned up, crushing Schopenhauer's fragile ego. He never completed his scheduled lectures, and dropped out of academia altogether, something he blamed on Hegel for the next forty years. Hegel, meanwhile, flourished in Berlin society – becoming Rector of the University in 1829 – until his sudden death during a cholera epidemic in 1831.

As Berlin earned its place as a powerhouse in philosophy, it was also during this period that the city developed its prowess in engineering and began to industrialize at a swift pace. Tardy among European powers in industrialization, Germany had a latecomer's advantage in beginning with the most up-to-date technology. Britain may have had the first railways, but August Borsig, founded in 1837, became within thirty-odd years the largest locomotive producer in Europe. The next year, the first railway in Prussia was built between Berlin and Potsdam, and within a decade Berlin was one of Europe's largest railway hubs. A city that was so connected hardly needed walls, and the old Akzisemauer was torn down finally in 1866.

Towards the middle of the century, the population had almost tripled to approximately 400,000 inhabitants since 1800, with the wave of industrialization and city jobs. With this came a housing shortage and rising social problems. The lack of established spaces for workers to socialize created a neighbourhood of tents, called *In den Zelten* ('in the tents'),

This building is on the site of what was the Mendelssohn Residence on Leipziger Strasse.

A MIDSUMMER NIGHT'S DREAM

In a more private corner of Berlin, on a fine summer night in 1826, the seventeen-year-old Felix Mendelssohn was sitting in the new garden of his family's villa on Leipziger Strasse 3, where he intended to 'dream' his overture to *A Midsummer Night's Dream*. The sounds of the wind in the trees perhaps inspired him to jot down the first notes; perhaps the low sounds of insects and birds evoked the fairies of the Bard's play. The overture's instruments suggest other dramatis personae: the strings' 'hee-haw' braying of Bottom transformed into a donkey, and the fanfare announcing the royal court of Athens. The *Dream*'s 'Wedding March', is of course, one of the world's most recognized melodies. Now the Mendelssohn house is gone, replaced by a government building of the *Bundesrat* (or Federal Council), and Leipziger Strasse is a soulless thoroughfare leading to Potsdamer Platz. But one can still peek through the gates at the address, to the greenery behind, and imagine the garden house where the family staged concerts or 'Sunday musicales', with the young prodigy at the piano. Here, at the age of sixteen, he also composed his Octet for Strings, op. 20, as a birthday present for his violin teacher. What happened to this youthful genius? Mendelssohn, who produced his most beloved music as a teenager, became a full-grown man well known for his work in music conservation (his 'historical concerts'), looking – regretfully? – over his shoulder to the brilliance of the past.

along the Tiergarten, in what is now John-Foster-Dulles-Allee next to the House of World Cultures. The tenuous subsistence of workers would soon give rise to protest. It was under the rule of Friedrich Wilhelm IV (1795–1861) that there was finally an uprising in Silesia of textile workers (in 1844), followed in 1846 by an economic crisis and more mass poverty. In these conditions, an assassination attempt on the king was not surprising. Nor, following a poor harvest, was a Berlin food riot in April 1847 called the 'Potato Revolution'. It was fertile ground for rebellion, and the February revolution in Paris led to the March revolution in Berlin. As the much-quoted saying goes, 'When Paris sneezes, Europe catches cold.'

On 18 March 1848, two hundred Berliners were killed in street riots following the publication of their demands. In front of the Hohenzollern palace, and then in the streets, the military shot on the orders of the man who would eventually become the first king of a united Germany: 'Grapeshot' Prince Wilhelm (*Kartätschenprinz*). The victims' bodies were then laid out in front of the Baroque City Palace. After Friedrich Wilhelm IV had withdrawn the army, he bowed down before the dead in a moment of what was probably genuine contrition, speaking to his 'dear Berliners' of an 'unfortunate misunderstanding'. He even wore the colours of the revolution on his armband: the red, gold and black that would eventually become the colours of the flag of the German republic. Reform, however, would not be forthcoming. Despite the election of a National Assembly in May, concessions were quickly reversed, sealed by a restoration of power by force in November 1848 by the reactionary general Friedrich von Wrangel. Only the powerful would be favoured in the three-tier elections, set for May 1849. As the historian A.J.P. Taylor wrote, in 1848 Germany 'failed to turn'.

What story do we tell about Berlin in Prussia in light of the restoration of repressive and military rule, following the liberal advances of the eighteenth century and the legacy of the French invasion? Was the absence of subsequent revolutions in German history an important precondition for the rise of the Third Reich? Historians continue to debate whether militarism is the 'special path' of German history, or whether speaking of a 'path' is overly deterministic. Arguments about the Prussian past too conveniently anticipate the darkness that was to come. Prussian discipline is seen as a pernicious precursor to Nazism, rather than as a laudable culture of honesty, sense of duty and incorruptibility. Then again, Prussian discipline itself might be a myth. Carl von Clausewitz wrote in 1807 comparing the Germans and the French: 'one [nation] was militaristic, and the subject mentality of its people doomed them to political "obedience"; the other had a more literary bent, and its hyper-critical inhabitants would be unlikely to submit to tyranny.' The second group were the Germans.

Improvements to public space made Potsdamer Platz a popular meeting point. Soon its traffic would be so bad that such stately strolling across its roads, as depicted in this picture (*c.* 1900), would become impossible. On the left-hand side, notice an example of one of the *Litfass* advertising pillars admired by Mark Twain.

3 New World Capital (1871–1918)

Like many more recent arrivals, Mark Twain (1835–1910) came to Berlin in 1891 because he thought it would be cheap. Facing financial difficulties in Hartford, Connecticut, he ended up slumming it for six months with his family in an apartment in Körnerstrasse – in what is still a gritty corner of Schöneberg now spiced with sex shops – until he could no longer afford Berlin either. Nonetheless, he wrote that the city was remarkably clean and orderly. He was astonished at how new it looked ('the main mass of the city looks as if it had been built last week'), how spacious ('Berlin is not merely a city of wide streets, it is the city of wide streets'), how straight and level the streets were ('the chromo[lithography] for flatness of surface . . .') and how quickly it was growing ('. . . and phenomenal swiftness of growth). His final judgement compared the city to a fast-growing American metropolis: 'Berlin is the European Chicago.'

Indeed, in the late nineteenth century Berlin was startled by its sudden emergence as a world capital and industrial hub: its population increased from half a million to one million people between 1857 and 1871, and to two million by 1899, and these numbers did not include areas outside the city proper. In places, the population density was 60,000 per square kilometre. An influx of population came from territories to the east, connected to the capital by the excellent railway network, and the phrase 'a true Berliner is Silesian' became popular. The inhabited areas stretched out to the west, with factory spaces located farther east. Trade winds ensured that the western areas had better air. They also had pleasant lakes and forests that had attracted the Hohenzollerns to hunt. The west became the rich side of the city, and farmers became millionaires selling lakeside property here. But in the teeming centre, the proletarian boroughs spread out from Alexanderplatz to the north, east and south.

The Holbrecht master plan was set into motion from 1862 to deal with the problems of overpopulation and to draw an urban map for the new Berlin. The authoritarian role of the police superintendent remained important in implementing these changes. The housing boom that occurred during what was called the *Gründerzeit*, or 'foundation era', was phenomenal until the overheated economy slowed with the 1873 stock market crash.

The archetypal housing project of the age was the *Mietskaserne*, or 'rental barracks'. One explanation for the name was

Berliner *Mietskasernen*. 'Rental barracks' were the predominant building model in the late 19th century in Berlin.

Mietskasernen today, in Kreuzberg.

that Berlin had many soldiers who needed to be housed with private families. More likely, the name suggested how close together the housing blocks were built and how very full they became. Five-storey-high houses, adorned with decorative plaster reliefs that could be chosen from a catalogue, stretched far back from the street fronts through a series of courtyards whose minimum size (5.34 square metres) was determined by the operation of a rolling fire pump. The building had a class structure: the *Vorderhaus*, or 'Front House', was for the affluent. The richer you were, the fewer stairs you had to climb, with the wealthiest occupying the first-floor *Bel Étage*. Further back, the 'Garden House' was for the poorer occupants. The 'garden' would more likely be occupied by stables and workshops. The apartments could be fitted with elaborate coal furnaces; a system of approximately one thousand water pumps and fountains had already been installed throughout the city by 1856, along with gasworks.

The *Mietskaserne* soon developed a reputation for causing sickness and disease. Mark Twain may not have seen enough back courtyards to qualify his opinion of the orderly city, although it is hard to believe that he missed what an aristocratic family noticed in Theodor Fontane's novel *Effi Briest*.

The stairwell of a *Mietskaserne* in Kreuzberg.

Fontane recounts his protagonists' apartment search in Berlin in the 1880s. They go

> to the vicinity of the Zoo, to look for an apartment in that area. And as it happened they did locate something eminently suitable in Keithstrasse, which was where they had been thinking of from the outset, except that it was a new building, damp and not quite finished. 'It won't do, Effi dear,' said Frau von Briest, 'it must be ruled out simply for health reasons. You don't put in a Privy Councillor to dry out plaster.'

And indeed, the stately Frau von Briest is astute in identifying a major risk of the fast housing boom. Families that occupied apartments before they were quite ready had a high rate of infant mortality, as children suffered when exposed to wet plaster that needed three months to dry.

Heinrich Zille (1858–1929), called a *Rinnstein-Künstler*, or 'gutter artist', by the emperor, is the famous illustrator of the less elegant side of the *Mietskaserne*, with his Baudelairian perspective on the poetry of the underclass. His lithographs are claustrophobic, a testament to the overcrowding of proletarian life. In fetid interiors, toddlers tumble from tables, men are habitually slumped unconscious from drink and women with satirically broad backsides disrobe, while every human function from sex to defecation happens in close quarters.

Berlin's sanitation was horrific in the early 1800s, and this problem continued well into the century. Since cesspits, located in the back courtyards, were expensive to empty, many simply dumped their chamber pots in the streets, and the contents then washed into the groundwater and river, causing sickness such as cholera. A sexist joke of the period played on the pun of *Berlinerinnen* (women of Berlin), which sounded the same as *Berliner Rinnen* (gutters of Berlin). It went as follows: 'A foreigner, visiting Berlin for the first time, was asked whether he liked the city. "The city is on the whole very nice," he replied, "But the women of Berlin (*Berliner*(*R*)*innen*) stink something awful."' Meanwhile, even more luxurious establishments, such as the Royal Opera

Heinrich Zille's depiction of overcrowding in Berlin homes, in *Geburtstag* (Birthday, 1909).

House, shocked foreigners with their reliance on chamber pots. Twain timed his stay correctly, arriving as improvements were completed. Europe's most modern sewers were finally built from 1873 to 1893, something badly needed to ameliorate the crowded, and often gloomy, unsanitary conditions inside the *Mietskasernen*'s back courtyards. Twelve *Radialsysteme*, or pumping stations, dealt with the city's wastewater – the fifth *Radialsystem* has now been converted into an innovative arts space near Ostbahnhof, and there is no trace that it managed decades of city excrement. Soon enough the *Mietskasernen* were massively improved, the most emblematic being the complex at the 1906 Hackesche Höfe, with its many courtyards built in response to the ghastly public health situation elsewhere. It was a model *Mietskaserne*, with its baths, proper heating and plumbing.

Electrification was yet another achievement of the period, with Berlin's first electric lights installed in Pariser Platz in 1878. Much of Berlin's success in this field was powered by its industrial concerns: Borsig, Siemens and AEG, who supplied the first electric tram (1881) and Berlin's S-Bahn (1882) and U-Bahn (1902) with power. The first cars were registered in the 1890s, and planning for a racetrack (AVUS, which was also the prototype for the Autobahn) began in 1907. Berlin was already a railway hub, but it soon opened an airport too, at Johannisthal.

Industrialization, and Berlin's growing position as the capital of a strong Continental power, brought population, and this brought consumption and amusements. Advertising pillars (*Litfass*) were built around Berlin, and these curiosities caught Twain's attention: 'One generally finds a group around each pillar reading these things. There are plenty of things in Berlin worth importing to America. It is these that I have particularly wished to make a note of.' He also was impressed by the number of city newspapers: 'There is an abundance of newspapers in Berlin . . . At intervals of half a mile on the thoroughfares there are booths, and it is at these that you buy your papers.' The *Morgenpost* dates from Twain's era, and the *Berliner Zeitung* would be inaugurated in 1904.

The department store played an important role in taking women out of the home and putting them independently into what was considered a respectable public space. The 24,000-square-metre Kaufhaus des Westens (KaDeWe) opened in 1907 and transformed the residential street where it was located, Tauentzienstrasse, into a luxurious boulevard. *Der Tauentzien* became a byword for all that was commercially spectacular about the capital. The German-Jewish composer Willy Rosen (1894–1944, killed in Auschwitz) would later enthuse about everything in Berlin from the street lamps to the women, from KaDeWe to the omnibus to Halensee, singing: 'the whole world is beautiful, but only one street in the whole Empire is simply smashing.' Both KaDeWe and Wertheim (1897, on Leipziger Strasse), which became two of the largest department stores in Europe, were owned by Jewish families.

Jewish Berliners in the Empire entered into a period of mass acculturation to the codes of the German gentile majority. The Jewish population of Berlin had increased from 3,000 to 45,000 between 1812 and 1874, a population boom driven by the arrival of poorer immigrants from the east (*Ostjuden*). Many wealthier Jews sought to distance themselves from these new arrivals, turning away from orthodoxy, whose traditions were often subject to stereotype and derision. The concept of *Bildung*, education in high culture, became the sought-after entrance ticket to German society – the idea, following the Mendelssohn model, that Jews would find acceptance if they were leaders in German culture.

The German-Jewish impressionist Max Liebermann (1847–1935) painted acculturated bourgeois life in his villa on the shores of a lake, Wannsee, just a few doors down from where the notorious Conference was held in 1942. His work idealizes German culture, and is, in fact, the epitome of bourgeois Berlin life, with his depictions of white-frocked tennis players by the sea, horse racing and promenades through manicured public parks. The historian Fritz Stern calls Jewish–German relations at the end of the nineteenth century 'symbiotic', pointing to an increased level of intermarriage, and Jewish

Berlin's Italian community was famous for its street organ production. This organ is kept in Berlin's Märkisches Museum.

THE FIRST ITALIANS IN BERLIN

New population brought new diversity to the *Mietskaserne* block housing projects. The freshly built borough of Prenzlauer Berg, for example, became an island of North Italian immigration between Schönhauser Allee and Pappelallee dedicated to the production of pipe instruments (*Drehorgelbau*). By 1890, fifty workers were busy making grinder organs at Cocchi Bacigalupo & Galligna on Schönhauser Allee 78. An Italian colony, including restaurants, grew up, and instrument production continued until 1975, in the GDR. The organs were originally popular with beggars who played them in public places, and the courtyards of the *Mietskasernen*, for money. And in the impoverished aftermath of the First World War, many veterans were organ grinders until the Nazis outlawed begging. I first stumbled across this peculiar strand of Prenzlauer Berg history when I was in the *Zócalo*, or Central Square, of Mexico City, where, in the poverty of that teeming metropolis, I saw an organ grinder. I approached her and asked her why the surprising address 'Schönhauser Allee' was written on her instrument. She was unable to tell me how the organ – piping German *Lieder* – had made its journey across the Atlantic to the New World. But years later, I stumbled across a room in the Märkisches Museum dedicated to these Italian immigrants and filled with many organs, and solved part of the puzzle that had presented itself in Mexico: the history of these curious instruments' production.

successes in the arts and sciences. But it is hard today not to see these achievements through the lens of the coming destruction. Late in life, Liebermann eventually wrote, in a letter to the mayor of Tel Aviv Meir Dizengoff in 1933, 'The abolition of equality haunts us like a terrible nightmare, especially those Jews like me who believed in the dream of assimilation.'

The dizzying expansion of Berlin was in the context of the massive expansion of Germany itself. The architect of these political changes was the Prussian minister Otto von Bismarck, born in a village a hundred kilometres to the west of Berlin. He distrusted the big city, and many of his social policies were intended to placate the growth of unions in Berlin's 'red' industrial heart, who saw themselves among the inheritors of the spirit of 1848. Here we see once again the forces of revolution and counter-revolution pitted against one another, but with the latter in firm control. Marching into battle, adorned with military insignia, the orange band of the Black Eagle Order and an azure coat, Bismarck was famously a proponent of *Realpolitik* – a politics of power and manipulation according to which the ends justify the means. In the 1890s he wrote of his war of 'defence' against the French, who were defeated at Sedan in 1870, that 'success depends essentially upon the impression . . . that we should be the ones attacked.' Bismarck, for all his military ambition, was also very careful, both abroad and at home.

The war with the French facilitated German unification by rallying all the various German states – such as Catholic Bavaria, Hesse-Darmstadt and Baden, but not Austria – to a unified battle against a common enemy. Germany was first declared a unified empire not on home ground, but in France. The Hall of Mirrors at Versailles saw the crowning of Wilhelm I, the erstwhile 'Grapeshot Prince', in 1871. Germany now stretched from Alsace and Lorraine in the west to the Eastern Baltic, and from Denmark to the Alps, in a territory that was a third larger (almost 200,000 square kilometres) than its present area. Germany's growing colonial ambitions were discussed at the Berlin Conference of 1884, as Germany's power extended into Cameroon, Togo and present-day

Tauentzienstrasse: a view of Berlin's *flâneur* promenade in 1903.

Namibia, all of which would be lost within little more than a generation.

Berlin was, for many, the parvenu capital of a parvenu country. The city already had a new Red City Hall (Rotes Rathaus, completed in 1869), but new symbols were needed for its exalted national status. It needed a parliament, which met first in an old porcelain manufacturers on Leipziger Strasse, whose roof was in such bad repair that shards would fall from it, endangering the members below. The Reichstag building, built in 1894, must have been very welcome. The Victory Column (*Siegessäule*) was the most important of these symbolic structures, crowned by *Goldelse*, a sculpture of Victory, and wreaths made from the metal of enemy cannons. Originally in front of the Reichstag, and later placed by the Nazis in the middle of the Tiergarten, it was inaugurated in

1873 and depicts the numerous German victories that rallied Germanic peoples in their common nationalist cause against their external enemies, including wars against Denmark (1864) and Austria (1866). It has acquired new meanings over time, especially for Berlin's gay community, who have 'demilitarized' the phallic monument, making it the end-point of the gay pride parade and the name of the local gay magazine.

It was Queen Victoria's grandson, the compulsive hunter and tree cutter Wilhelm II, Germany's troubled successor to Kaiser Wilhelm I, who was most responsible for upsetting Bismarck's carefully constructed balances of power with its neighbours. And with him, and the stumbling machinations of the other European powers, Berlin's fortunes tumbled into the largely unexpected and catastrophic defeat of the First World War. Two-thirds of the eleven million men mobilized by Germany in the First World War would become casualties, most dying in the slow war of attrition fought in the trenches of the Western Front.

One of the most remarkable anecdotes from the period must be the visit of sharpshooter Annie Oakley's *Buffalo Bill's Wild West Show* to Berlin in 1889, when the blustering Kaiser Wilhelm II reputedly jumped on stage, offering himself to the western star, to have her shoot the end off his cigarette. Did she almost change the course of European history? Oakley endorsed the story after the First World War began, writing to the Kaiser and asking if she might have a second shot.

4 Desperation and Decadence (1918–1933)

After the horrors of the First World War came massive societal change. Berlin in the 1920s is legendary, but there is more than one legend. For some, it is the decade of failure, proven by its doomed democracy's sinister end-point: the Third Reich. It was a time of grinding poverty and political divisiveness. And yet, this portrait of a Germany disgraced, forced into unwilling atonement by the Versailles Treaty, is one side of the coin. It is in stark contrast to the other story told about this decade in Berlin: that of the *Goldene Zwanziger*, or Golden Twenties. During this era the city became a dynamic metropolis, a city of remarkable artistic production and sexual freedom. Perhaps one might reconcile these stories by arguing that instability inspired creative responses. However, much of the artistic explosion came in a period of stabilization, reigniting the debate over 'Weimar Berlin' once again.

Berlin was the pivot of many of the turning points of Weimar Germany's three phases: the brutal post-war political and economic struggles, the subsequent stabilization and the final crisis ignited by the 1929 market crash (which we will look at in the next chapter). It was in Berlin that, on 9 November 1918, two visions for a new Germany were proclaimed. The Social Democrats (SPD) announced the 'German Republic' from the Reichstag, while the far-left *Spartakusbund*, which would become the Communist Party of Germany (KPD), declared a 'German Free Socialist Republic' from the Berlin City Palace. Wilhelm II abdicated in late November, ending half a millennium of Hohenzollern rule.

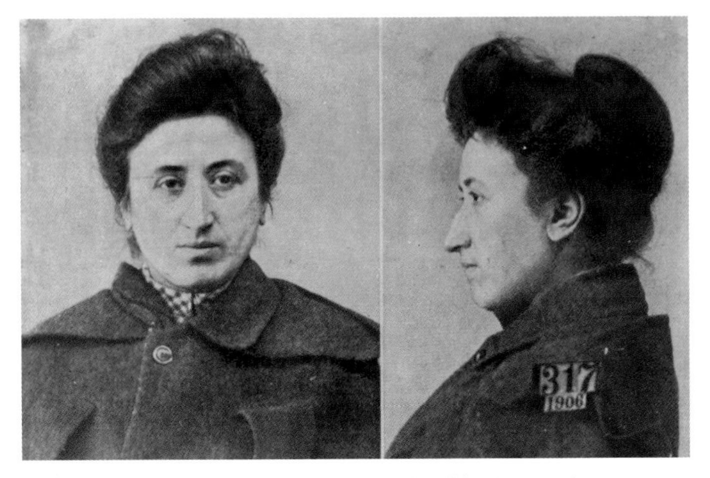

Rosa Luxemburg, murdered in 1919, was a leader of the Communist *Spartakus* League.

Legions of traumatized and unemployed soldiers had meanwhile filled Berlin. Hans Fallada, in his novel *Iron Gustav*, recalled the scene of war wounded along Friedrichstrasse in this period: 'Armless and legless – trousers pushed up to show the thick purple or red scabs on the stumps – there they sat, the mutilated, those with faces terribly scarred and burnt, those with missing jaws – horror upon horror.' Many more able-bodied veterans, dispirited and nostalgic for the days of the Kaiser, proposed traditional and authoritarian solutions for Germany's problems. They joined *Freikorps* paramilitary organizations, precursors to the Nazi SA and SS.

The SPD government colluded with the *Freikorps* to control the workers' uprising that followed the twin declarations of 9 November. On 15 January 1919 the *Spartakus* leaders, Karl Liebknecht and Rosa Luxemburg, were shot in the Tiergarten. Her body was dumped into the Landwehr Canal, probably while she was still alive. More than a thousand Berliners died in those first months of 1919. The complicity of the SPD with the *Freikorps* would divide the left, later preventing it from launching a united front against the Nazis, who would find many recruits among the former soldiers. Rosa Luxemburg became a martyr of the left, and 1919 is remembered as the moment when revolution almost made Berlin the capital of a Communist Germany. There would be another opportunity.

At this time Ludwig Finckh, the popular novelist and physician, and friend of Hermann Hesse, wrote disparagingly of the capital in a Stuttgart daily:

> Berlin is not Germany. Berlin is not even Prussia. There are many good Prussians who want nothing to do with it. We in southern Germany will no longer go along with it . . . Everything is topsy-turvy there; guns go off on their own, wolves have been turned into deer . . . Another must oppose the spirit of Berlin, and that is the spirit of Germany!

This regionalism is familiar to Berliners today, who consider themselves as living on a libertine island in a stereotyped sea of German *Spiessigkeit*, or square provinciality, given to reactionary politics. (Finckh, incidentally, became an active member of the Nazi Party from 1933 and head of propaganda in his lakeside town near the Swiss border, giving lectures on Nazi race theory; he would later be tried as a 'minor offender' in a denazification trial.) The *Freikorps* soon had their own uprising in Berlin, with the March 1920 Kapp Putsch, taking control of the city for a short time until being squashed by a massive general strike. Berlin in the years that followed became a hotbed of underground tension and the capital of political assassinations, with almost five hundred politicians dead by the middle of the decade.

The radicalization of politics was followed by the hyperinflation of 1923, exacerbated by a missed reparations payment imposed by the punitive Treaty of Versailles of 1919. It brought industrial strike action, and with it Germany came to the edge of total economic collapse (the trauma resulting from this remains a force in European politics even today, with a fearful Germany accused of actually promoting deflation in the Eurozone). A stabilization plan put into effect by November

The hyperinflation of 1923 continues to haunt German public finances.

HYPERINFLATION IN BERLIN

One of the greatest financial failures in history is Germany's inability to control inflation during and after the First World War. An ineffective taxation regime, runaway expenditure and a readiness to print money all put Germany in a poor position when confronting the post-war burden of paying reparations. Inflation had already begun during the war, but between January and November 1923, it skyrocketed. The price of bread in Berlin increased by 804 million per cent during that period. Bartering became widespread, those on fixed incomes faced disaster and employees often renegotiated their wages at the beginning of a shift only to find they had worked for nothing by day's end. A haircut was valued in numbers of eggs, and a doctor's visit in wine and butter. Wheelbarrows and suitcases were used to deliver money; the former were stolen, and the latter abandoned or used to wallpaper bathrooms. Betty Scholem, writing to her son in Switzerland from Berlin in October 1923, explained: 'Conditions have taken a catastrophic turn here. Notice that this letter cost 15 million cash; it will be 30 million beginning the day after tomorrow – and this price will most likely last a mere two days at most.' This chaotic world proved an opportunity for some. Victims included those who saved, or who sold to speculators dabbling in gold and silver, foreign exchange or property. The novelist Stefan Zweig recalled later: 'To describe the hyperinflation, with all its incredible details, would require me to write a book, and people today would take this book as a fairy tale . . . For one hundred dollars, you could buy rows of six-storey houses on the Kurfürstendamm. Factories could be had for the equivalent of what a wheelbarrow had once cost.'

1923 – with subsequent deals on reparations and debt – led, remarkably, to a half-decade of relative normality between 1924 and 1929.

In this period of tremendous political change, the shape of Berlin also changed radically. On 27 April 1920 a new Berlin city law had come into effect which made surrounding towns and villages part of the city of Berlin. This legislation added over a million people to Berlin's population, bringing the total to close to four million, more than today. The city, along with Paris, became the joint largest on the Continent. Many western areas, which were richer and more politically conservative, were included, but a quarter of the population in 1929 was still living on social assistance. In poorer neighbourhoods to the east there was an effort, in the period of stabilization, to increase social housing alternatives. A number of these housing estates, in the Berlin Modern style, are now included on the UNESCO World Heritage List.

Berlin was known, at least comparatively to other cities, for its tempo. The traffic whirring through Potsdamer Platz with Europe's first ever traffic lights (1925), the founding of Lufthansa in Berlin (1926), Tempelhof Airport (1927) and the mass transit system unified under the BVG (Berliner Verkehrsbetriebe, 1928) were all symbols of the capital's invigorated pace. The enormous pride in the interconnected transport system is best seen in a viewing of the Walter Ruttmann film *Berlin: Symphony of a Great City* (1927), a ballet of public conveyances.

That said, plenty of Berliners preferred to walk, and perhaps the most famous *flâneur* was Franz Hessel, who captured the feeling of street life. He laments, however, that 'my dear fellow Berliners don't make it easy for me, no matter how deftly I nip around them. I always get suspicious looks whenever I stroll among the industrious. I think they must take me for a pickpocket.' Others preferred the slow pace of a boat. Billy Wilder's first major success as a screenwriter was with the film *People on Sunday* (1930), which showed an unvarnished outing of two couples, played by amateur actors, who escape the city's frenetic speed by visiting a Berlin lake on a Sunday. There is a focus on the intimate – faces uplit by lake water – and one of the most poignant aspects of the film is seeing children playing who would be of military age just a decade later.

Artistic life in musical culture was also in the ascendancy. Ferruccio Busoni's leadership at the Prussian Academy of the Arts (Preussische Akademie der Künste) was taken over in 1925 by Arnold Schoenberg, who wrote music using his twelve-tone system. In the same year, Alban Berg premiered his scandalous but successful *Wozzeck* at the Berlin State Opera. Paul Hindemith was made a professor at the Berliner Hochschule in 1927; his *Gebrauchsmusik*, or 'utility music', like Carl Orff's music education programme, would later become entangled in the Nazi project.

Kurt Weill was a Busoni student whose *Threepenny Opera*, with its naturalist libretto written by Bertolt Brecht, premiered at the Theater am Schiffbauerdamm in 1928. Its world of pimps,

Haus Vaterland, in Potsdamer Platz, was a theme park of international restaurants, the world's largest café and a cinema. It could be considered the forefather of Epcot. This image is from 1932.

Clärchens Ballhaus is a dance hall that first opened in Mitte in 1913 and was popular in the Weimar era among Zille, Döblin and the arts scene.

beggars and underground criminality – and that famous ballad about 'Mack the Knife' – although set in nineteenth-century London, was familiar enough to the embattled Berliners of the 1920s. Like Hindemith, Weill focused on practical, everyday applications for contemporary classical music; he even penned a quite ferocious attack on elitist composers who had no connection to the social and political problems of Berlin's public. Schoenberg notoriously annotated Weill's article of 1927, putting a big X on the page and critically underlining the words 'understand' and 'understandable', highlighting the two composers' opposing notions regarding the social engagement of music.

In the visual arts, the inheritors of the counterculture spirit of the Berliner Secession moved into Expressionism, with the lurid street scenes of Ernst Ludwig Kirchner (1880–1938) and the group Die Brücke. The sardonic political criticism of George Grosz and Otto Dix, and other figures whom you might find sitting in the arty Romanisches Café, led the New Objectivity (*Neue Sachlichkeit*) style. In film the UFA theatres were famous for promoting dystopic social worlds, especially in Fritz Lang's *Metropolis* (1927). The sexually frank, glamorous underworld of Marlene Dietrich meanwhile was the dive-bar antithesis to the wild open spaces of the mountain films of G. W. Pabst, which starred an ambitious young woman named Leni Riefenstahl (who hated Marlene). Riefenstahl would soon capture the imagination of Adolf Hitler.

Berlin's literary landscape was also gritty and naturalistic in character, typified by the adventures among Berlin's whore-houses and bars of Ernst Kästner's *Fabian* (1931), the desperate juvenile gang culture of Ernst Haffner's *Blood Brothers* (1932), and the seedy wanderings of a released prisoner in Alfred Döblin's *Berlin Alexanderplatz* (1929).

The novelist Christopher Isherwood did plenty to promote this gritty, sexy image of Berlin excitement in the English-speaking world. The Cambridge dropout's 'docu-fiction' memoirs, *Mr Norris Changes Trains* (1935) and *Goodbye to Berlin* (1939), based on his time living in Berlin between 1929 and 1933, later inspired the musical *Cabaret* (and the film adaptation starring Liza Minnelli of 1972). Isherwood created the attractively degraded figure of Sally Bowles, who for many has become a caricature of the entire period. The naive but naughty cabaret singer is described by her 'fingernails, [which] were painted emerald green, a colour unfortunately chosen, for it called attention to her hands, which were much stained by cigarette smoking and as dirty as a little girl's'. Isherwood for his part later said that Berlin was boring because nobody had any money. Nonetheless, he and his friends did seem to have had plenty of amusement; they 'came for the boys', as relatively privileged sex tourists adventuring in a city with massive levels of unemployment, the vulnerable world that so engaged Weill, Kirchner and Kästner.

Irmgard Keun's novel *The Artificial Silk Girl* (1932), banned by the Nazis, describes one of Berlin's victims. When Doris first arrives in Berlin, to the rush of Friedrichstrasse station, she is swept up in a crowd that carries her up Unter den Linden to the Hotel Adlon. There, from below a balcony, she sees the French premier and foreign minister on a state visit, waving to a mass reception below. Her impressions of being absorbed by the city follow:

> Everything turned into a scream and the masses swept over me . . . and I was shouting with them, because so many voices pierced through my body that they came back out of my mouth. And I had this idiotic crying fit, because I was so moved. And I immediately belonged to Berlin, being right in the middle of it – that pleased me enormously. And the politicians lowered their heads in a statesmanly fashion, and so, in a way, they were greeting me too.

Doris's poignant self-delusion about her importance in the rush of the city foreshadows her impending descent into grinding poverty and sexual exploitation – the fate of so many young people who came to the city.

The state's concern with the birth rate after the First World War stimulated research on reproduction and sexual health. Berlin became the world centre of sex research, armed with new developments in contraception. While homosexuality was officially illegal, legislation was rarely enforced (unlike in the United Kingdom). Germany's gay rights movement, active since the 1890s, gained steam with a bill of legalization brought forward in 1929. It was the Nazis who would put a stop to such innovations, and they shut down Magnus Hirschfeld's well-known Institute for Sexual Research, shortly after the infamous book burning in Bebelplatz of May 1933.

The Nazis' coming attack on difference would be most felt in the Jewish community. One of the most poignant moments in Christopher Isherwood's *Goodbye to Berlin* is the character Christopher's encounter with a family, the fictional Landauers, based on the real-world Israels, who ran a department store, Kaufhaus N. Israel, located near the Red City Hall close to Alexanderplatz. Like other Jewish businesses, it would be 'Aryanized' after *Kristallnacht* in 1938. Christopher gives English lessons to the daughter in the Landauers' Grunewald home and observes their secular family life. The father is eager to impress his open-mindedness on Christopher by querying him about Oscar Wilde. The Landauers' son, Bernhard, is an enigmatic figure described as both Jewish and German, with perhaps 'one drop of pure Prussian blood in [his] polluted veins'.

Wealthy and acculturated, Bernhard, however, is 'ultimately doomed'; the character will eventually die euphemistically of 'heart failure' under the Nazis.

At their last meeting, Bernhard teases Christopher with the idea that they leave Germany together, but immediately, 'this evening', to China by way of the Trans-Siberian Railway. Christopher at first takes Bernard's 'most daring and most cynical experiment' in jest. He can't accept; he has his washing to pick up. He asks his friend, 'Can't it wait until tomorrow?' Bernhard replies, 'Tomorrow is too late.' It is more than a year later that Christopher realizes the radical offer to leave Berlin together – the only kind that would have saved Bernhard's life – was in fact 'perfectly serious'.

On the day of Hitler's seizure of power, 30 January 1933, paramilitaries assembled at the Brandenburg Gate.

5 Nazi Berlin (1933–1939)

A young man walking home hears the sound of breaking glass and alerts the police. A policeman inspects the building and sees flames. The maid of the head of the Nazi Press Office sees the fire from her window and rouses her master, the *mondain* Ernst 'Putzi' Hanfstängl, who immediately calls Joseph Goebbels to tell him the Reichstag is on fire. But Goebbels hangs up because he thinks it is a joke. Rudolf Diels, head of what would be renamed the Gestapo, arrives to interrogate the confused 24-year-old Dutch Communist Marinus van der Lubbe, dragged from the burning building. Diels later recounted how Lubbe was 'naked from the waist upwards, smeared with dirt and swearing . . . he panted as if he had completed a tremendous task. There was a wild, triumphant gleam in the burning eyes of his pale, haggard young face.' And although Lubbe appeared to have acted alone, when the Nazi elite arrived to observe the 'red sea of flames', they considered the act of arson a Communist revolt. Hitler

> shouted uncontrollably, as I had never seen him do it before, as if he was going to burst: 'There will be no mercy now. Anyone who stands in our way will be cut down. The German people will not tolerate leniency. Every Communist official will be shot where he is found.'

The fire gave Hitler his national emergency. While many of Hitler's methods had been illegal, he was ultimately able to exploit weaknesses within the democratic system to destroy it. In this case, he seized upon Article 48 of the

Germany's seat of government, the Reichstag, site of an infamous arson attack in February 1933.

Weimar Constitution, which gave him emergency powers. With them, he moved swiftly to consolidate absolute power, for a total coordination of German society, or *Gleichschaltung* ('getting on the same gear'), in the service of his party and the *Volksgemeinschaft* (or 'people's community').

The Nazi Party had enjoyed a meteoric rise, building up its base from just 2.6 per cent federally in the 1928 elections. Goebbels was entrusted with the mission to entrench the Nazis into Berlin political life, and in 1926 he was appointed the city's *Gauleiter*. Hitler gave his first public Berlin speech in late 1928, and that year the Nazis won thirteen seats in the Berlin City Assembly, a gift from a public outraged by a corruption scandal. Alfred Hugenberg's Berlin press empire was meanwhile instrumental in publicizing the Nazi cause, and technology – the arrival of radio from 1923, and the building of the Funkturm (radio tower) in 1926 – provided yet new weapons for political propaganda. Street battles between Nazis and Communists became a regular feature of city life, beginning in March 1927 and with the 'Blood May' of 1929. In the Berlin streets, this created an atmosphere of instability, fomented purposely by the Nazis – so that the Nazis themselves could provide a solution, offering the public authority and security.

It was with the October 1929 stock market crash that mass unemployment again engulfed the capital; the rate rose from 1.3 million to 6 million across Germany from 1929 to 1933. This crisis was the Nazis' chance, building off nostalgia for the authoritarian and supposedly stable world before the Versailles Treaty. It is important, however, to remember that the city remained 'red', and, like Bismarck, Hitler could not count on Berlin. In the July 1932 elections, the Nazis received 28.6 per cent of the vote in Berlin (compared to 37.4 per cent nationally). Only after Hitler seized power and became Chancellor did Berlin vote slightly more in favour of the Nazis, with 42 per cent in the 5 March 1933 elections. But in this vote, which can be called neither free nor fair, more Berliners still supported the Communists.

Hitler's appointment as Chancellor, on 30 January 1933, was greeted by a mass parade of torches in front of the Brandenburg Gate by the party faithful. Max Liebermann apparently complained it was a pity that he could not eat as much as he'd like to vomit. These supporters, after the Reichstag fire, roamed through the courtyards of the *Mietskasernen*, hunting down ten thousand political opponents in the next two months. This round-up brought into existence the first concentration camps for those in so-called 'protective custody'. Hitler confirmed his authority with the 23 March 1933 Enabling Act, and in a little over a year his party was purged of 'enemies' from within. The Night of the Long Knives, on 30 June 1934, eliminated the SA's leadership – an event which the American ambassador to Berlin, William Dodd, compared to the French Terror. Many of the victims were first interrogated in the complex on Prinz-Albrecht-Strasse, which contained the Gestapo and SS headquarters, and became the most feared address in Berlin. It is now the location of the Topography of Terror exhibit.

Hitler meant to transform Germany, and also the city of Berlin. There is some debate as to how much Hitler hated Berlin. On the one hand, Berlin was the capital of his opponents: the city had never voted for Hitler, and it had long been the centre of Communist insurrection and threat. But on the other, Berlin also provided Hitler with his opportunity: it represented the decadence, both political and moral, that he wished to correct. He quickly went about centralizing power in the city and remaking it. 'Hitler is Germany and Germany is Hitler' became rephrased later in popular tracts: 'Berlin is the Reich, and the Reich is Berlin.' He had in mind a grand new architectural project.

The city would be renamed 'Germania', fashioned as a world capital, the old Berlin replaced by a grand plan of Nazi architecture engineered by Hitler's chief architect Albert Speer, to be finished by 1950. The model of the city took up a whole room in his office on Pariser Platz. Buildings, inspired by the Italian fascist examples, were in the style of stripped-down Neoclassicism, with high narrow windows, heavy casings, trim columns without capitals, a sense of verticality meant to make one feel small under the edifices' politicized shadow. The largest would be a Great Hall with room for 180,000 people. These buildings had their ends in mind, what Speer called their 'ruin value': they were designed to decay into attractive ruins so that archaeologists might admire the remains of a thousand-year *Reich*, or empire, just as they admired those of the Romans. Ironically, Hitler's rule would last only thirteen years, and a combination of bombing and Soviet dynamite would be sufficient to remove most traces of the Nazi imprint from Berlin's architecture. The 1934 Reichsbank, which now houses the German Foreign Ministry, is one of the few surviving administrative buildings from the period. The Nazi Ministry of Aviation is another notable illustration and houses the current Ministry of Finance, a history not lost on contemporary demonstrators against Germany's austerity policies. The expansion to the Tempelhof airfield, Fehrbelliner Platz, the ring-Autobahn around Berlin and the Olympic Stadium are other examples. The Nazis, meanwhile, underinvested in infrastructure for the poor; there was a

The Nazi Ministry of Aviation, built in 1936. It is now the Federal Ministry of Finance.

continued housing crisis. Very little remains of Speer's own works: his most monumental undertaking was Hitler's New Chancellery building, completed between 1938 and 1939 (costing more than €1 billion in today's coin). It was built in blood-red Saalburg marble that can still be seen reused today in the nearby Mohrenstrasse U-Bahn station, the foyer of the Volksbühne theatre, the entrance to the Humboldt University and at the Soviet War Memorial in Treptower Park. The GDR was meticulous in levelling the entire complex along Wilhelmstrasse – the government quarter roughly between the Brandenburg Gate and Potsdamer Platz – and built on it collective housing blocks and parking. Of Speer's works in Berlin, only four small temple-like structures surrounding the perimeter of the Victory Column remain, now converted into public conveniences, so visitors can actually shit on Nazi architecture.

In the world of the arts, meanwhile, the Nazis moved to suppress atonality, abstraction and Expressionism. The Berlin Philharmonic began to be Aryanized once it came to depend on public funds in October 1933, and radio, theatre and every other possible form of cultural life were brought to heel under Goebbels and his Propaganda Ministry. Artists who depended on large infrastructure and studios, such as those in film production, were more likely to stay, while those who worked in private, such as authors – including Bertolt Brecht, Alfred Döblin, Thomas Mann and Erich Maria Remarque – were more likely to emigrate. As the historian Richard Evans wrote, 'By the end of 1933, there was scarcely a writer of any talent or reputation left in Germany.' Berlin, as Germany's literary capital, saw a bloodletting of talent. The quality of the productions that remained was typified by sycophantic works such as the play *Schlageter*, by Hanns Johst, about a German uprising against the French in the 1920 Ruhr Valley. It opened for Hitler's 44th birthday on 20 April 1933, in the Schauspielhaus on Gendarmenmarkt, with the leader in the audience. The play made famous the line, which, for many, as a misquote, sums up the Nazi approach to the arts: 'When I hear the word culture, I reach for my gun!'

The Nazi aesthetics of classical architectural 'purity' and power, and degeneracy, can be mapped closely onto the racial aims of the state. On 1 April 1933 a massive boycott of Jewish businesses occurred (Isherwood recounts his experience of making a purchase on principle at the N. Israel Kaufhaus). The civil service was purged in the same month. In 1935 the Nuremberg Laws came into effect, stripping German Jews of their citizenship. And a pinnacle of pre-war repression came with the 9 November 1938 *Kristallnacht* destruction of nine of twelve Berlin synagogues, and the devastation of a thousand Jewish stores in the city. The historian Peter Gay recounts his Jewish childhood in Berlin, and how, at the age of fifteen, biking down the boulevard of commerce on Tauentzienstrasse on 10 November, he was confronted by the shop facades 'reduced to rubble, their huge display windows shattered, their mannequins and merchandise scattered on the sidewalk. I kept my head down and bicycled my way home.' Gay explains how the 1938 pogrom affected his father: 'at this moment a determination was born in him to do anything, no matter how illegal, to get the three of us away from the German nightmare.' Ejected from his school, Peter emigrated within a year.

For most Berliners, however, life in the 1930s was one of prosperity rather than terror, which might explain the low levels of civil protest. The Nazis had secured a large level of support at home, mostly because of their make-work projects. In February 1933, 20 per cent of Berliners were out of work, but by 1936 there was, in fact, a shortage of trained labour, with unemployment reduced sixfold by 1938. Meanwhile, GNP rose by 40 per cent between 1932 and 1937. While certain industries dried up, such as newspapers in the face of censorship and the purging of their Jewish journalists – three-quarters of all Berlin papers closed, including the popular *Vossische Zeitung* – metal industries (such as armaments) flourished. Berlin became Europe's most important industrial capital. This had its effect on the streets of Berlin, where the swastika was ubiquitous over full beer-gardens and busy shops. Indeed, life, in purely material terms, had massively improved since the 1920s, at least for those included in the racist definitions of the *Volksgemeinschaft*. The apotheosis of Berlin as Europe's greatest capital, according to the Nazis, was celebrated in 1937 with the 700th anniversary of the city, accompanied by a massive public exhibition celebrating Berlin's Germanic past and its position at the forefront of everything from film to atomic science.

The Berlin Olympics in 1936 were the Nazis' largest international publicity stunt. Germany had won the Olympic bid in 1931, before Hitler had come to power, and the Nazis' extreme politics posed a problem for the International Olympic Committee (IOC) because of the strong boycott movement promoted by Jewish groups in the United States. In the end, only the Soviet Union did not participate. Germany responded to the threat of a U.S. boycott by allowing German-Jewish athletes to participate, and relaxing anti-Jewish propaganda and prohibitions at home for the period of the games. An émigré German half-Jew living in California, Helene Mayer, was on the German fencing team, and, with a swastika on her

The East German TV series *Wolf Among Wolves* (1965), based on Hans Fallada's novel of 1937.

HANS FALLADA

Hans Fallada (born Rudolf Wilhelm Adolf Ditzen, 1893–1947) wrote his page-turner *Alone in Berlin* (*Jeder stirbt für sich allein*) in 1946, as a propaganda commission for the Soviet cultural authorities. His brief was to fictionalize how an old couple resisted the Nazis by dropping postcards with anti-Fascist messages around Berlin. Fallada was given the couple's police files, and he quickly produced an ambiguous story that shows both the Gestapo's brutality and the ineffectualness of the old couple's project, which only terrified those who found the cards. *Alone in Berlin* was first published in English in 2009, and the press seized on Primo Levi's endorsement of the 'greatest book written about the German resistance'. Fallada was also applauded for the time he had spent in prison under the Nazis. But few critics elucidated the ambiguous message of the novel or explained that Fallada had been committed to a psychiatric prison not for political activity, but for beating his wife. During the 1930s Fallada had enjoyed the patronage of a Nazi-controlled media company, Tobis, with whom he signed a contract for *Iron Gustav: A Berlin Family Chronicle* (1938). Again, he fictionalized a real-world subject, that of an old cabbie Gustav Hartmann (Iron Gustav Hackendahl in the novel), who in 1928 rode his coach from Berlin to Paris and back. Gustav's family's experiences between 1914 and 1933 became a vehicle for a nationalistic account of German history. Fallada was naive if he thought that he would not also be compelled to glorify the Nazis in this project, and he capitulated to Propaganda Minister Joseph Goebbels's demands that he amend his conclusion. Fallada, although he later wrote that he loathed what he did, eventually has the old cabbie join the Nazi party, with the words: 'Well then: let me come with you.' The English translation of 2014 is a triangulation of a heavily expurgated version of *Iron Gustav* published by Putnam in London in 1940 and a politically correct reconstruction from the GDR. The flurry of millennial Fallada-mania, following the success of *Alone in Berlin* – which exploited the myth of Fallada as a resistor, rather than exploring more critically the patronage of both the Nazis and the Soviets – may account for why the Nazi additions are not even included in the 2014 *Iron Gustav* appendix.

uniform, was awarded a silver medal, raising her right arm in a Nazi salute. Meanwhile, American black athletes won many medals, in a snub to Nazi racial pseudo-science, such as Jesse Owens, who returned home with four golds. When asked how he felt about the pervasive racism of Nazi Germany, and the fact that Hitler refused to shake his hand, Jesse Owens later replied that the American president did not shake his hand either.

The Olympics were documented by Leni Riefenstahl, the Berliner dancer, actress and film-maker who had already filmed the 1934 Nazi rally in Nuremberg. The games were a festival of Nazi aesthetics, propaganda and control. Just as Speer's architecture used classical examples to give legitimacy to the Nazi project, modelling it after ancient Rome, Riefenstahl depicted her athletes as classical statuary coming to life. The Olympics complex built in the far west of Berlin was sprawling and impressive, although Hitler was apparently disappointed by how small the stadium was, holding 100,000 spectators, the largest of its kind anywhere in the world. Riefenstahl was given an unlimited budget and developed in Berlin many of the techniques that are now standard in sports photography while celebrating athletic perfection and the body beautiful. She was later condemned by critics such as Susan Sontag for being 'the only major artist . . . whose work – not only during the Third Reich but thirty years after its fall – has consistently illustrated some of the themes of fascist aesthetics', exalting 'two seemingly opposite states, egomania and servitude'.

Berlin was utterly transformed by the Nazis, who ripped the guts out of the intelligentsia, scattering them across Europe and to the New World. The destruction of Jewish contributions to German life meant the destruction, in part, of German culture itself. Meanwhile, Berliners were rendered docile by material comforts and economic improvements, as well as by the terror of the Nazis' methods. Speer and Riefenstahl used luminous classical models to legitimize a Reich intended to fall into ruin. In fact it would not be long before the whole city would resemble the shell of the burnt-out Reichstag.

6 City of Murder (1939–1945)

William L. Shirer, an American press correspondent in Berlin since 1934, wrote in early September 1939:

> It has been a lovely September day, the sun shining, the air balmy, the sort of day the Berliner loves to spend in the woods or on the lakes nearby. I walked in the streets. On the faces of the people astonishment, depression . . . In 1914, I believe, the excitement in Berlin on the first day of the World War was tremendous. Today, no excitement, no hurrahs, no cheering, no throwing of flowers, no war fever, no war hysteria.

His *Berlin Diary* charts how little enthusiasm there was for war in Berlin before it started on 1 September, and how 'naïve and simple' the Berliner response to the war was once it had begun. Observing the Berliners' joyful reception of a military parade on Pariser Platz in July 1940, after the great victories in Western Europe, Shirer observed there was 'nothing martial about the mass of the people here', but he also

> wondered if any of them understood what was going on in Europe, if they had an inkling that their joy, that this victorious parade of the goose-steppers, was based on a great tragedy for millions of others whom these troops and the leaders of these people had enslaved. Not one in a thousand, I wager, gave the matter a thought.

Berlin Sportpalast, 18 February 1943, during Joseph Goebbels's 'Total War' speech.

On the one hand, Berlin would become the capital of an empire stretching from outside Moscow to the French Atlantic coast, from Crete to the Norwegian Arctic. On the other, it would become a self-regarding island again, relatively shielded from the excesses of war by propaganda and supply lines stretching far to the conquered territories of Europe, where millions were put to death. Shirer's accounts highlight the level of political apathy in the city, or wilful ignorance, regarding the fate of so many victims of the Nazi regime.

Only when the bombs began falling on Berlin, after 16 August 1940, did Berliners' naivety begin to disappear. They were stunned to be under attack, and only then did they begin turning off their radio broadcasts 'with that expressive Berlin exclamation: "Oh, *Quatsch*!" which is stronger than "Oh, nonsense!" "Rubbish" is probably a better translation.' It was in late 1943 that mass aerial bombing of the capital accelerated, culminating with the appalling destruction that accompanied the Soviet advance.

The great reversal of Germany's fortunes, and Berlin's morale, occurred at Stalingrad, where almost a million Axis troops lost their lives. Following the defeat, on 18 February

1943, Joseph Goebbels stood in the tense Sportpalast before a distraught but determined Berlin crowd. The walls of the cavernous Schöneberg ice rink were hung with swastikas, the quasi-religious symbols of the party. The slogan 'Total War – Shortest War' hung over 'a cross-section of German society . . . row on row of wounded soldiers from the Eastern Front, men with scarred bodies, with amputated legs or arms, men blinded in action.' And, in the shadow of defeat, the hyenine Propaganda Minister asked if they were 'resolved to follow the Führer through thick and thin, in the pursuit of victory, even if this should mean the heaviest of contributions?' This sacrifice is precisely what would be demanded of Berliners: within five years of the war's beginning, the densely populated metropolis would be a ruined shell of 90 million cubic metres of rubble. What a remarkable price Berliners paid for a war they entered with so little enthusiasm.

The focus on 'German' victims, however, must follow a discussion of the many more victims of Germans. After *Kristallnacht*, the majority of Jews remaining in the capital decided to leave. This might be seen as a metropolitan advantage: that in Berlin, closer to structures of power, and with plentiful international connections, there were fewer illusions about what the Nazis had in store. Of the approximately 170,000 Jews living in Berlin, 90,000 emigrated. Of those remaining, 62,000 would be killed, 7,000 would commit suicide and only 6,000 would survive. This destruction of the community happened in phases. In 1939 Jewish buildings were taken over and remaining businesses 'Aryanized'. Deportations began in earnest in 1941. It was in the lakeside suburb of Berlin at Wannsee, on 20 January 1942, that a logistical meeting took place; it was the implementation of a 'Final Solution' to exterminate Europe's Jewish community. By this point, only 15,000 Jews were still living in Berlin, mostly used as forced labour in factories, and the final major round-up occurred in late February 1943 during the *Fabrikaktion* (or Factory Operation). Eighteen hundred Jewish men were meanwhile held in a building on Rosenstrasse 2–4, while their non-Jewish German wives protested bravely outside for their freedom.

The workers of the Otto Weidt workshop.

After 9 September 1941 Jews could not go outside without identifying themselves by wearing a yellow Star of David. Nineteen-year-old Inge Deutschkron was one of the intrepid who defied the Nazi regulation; she would 'duck into a doorway, take off my coat, and put on a the jacket without a star that I carried with me. It was not an entirely risk-free procedure.' This subterfuge allowed her to use public transportation, visit her grocer and go to concerts. Deutschkron turned to the help of Otto Weidt, who employed approximately forty mostly blind and deaf Jews in his atelier, where they produced brushes and brooms that were sold to the Wehrmacht. He protected them from deportation until the *Fabrikaktion*. Weidt later went to Auschwitz to demand his workers back. One can still visit his workshop, now a small museum at Rosenthaler Strasse 39 in Mitte. Deutschkron meanwhile hid with her mother after 1943 and survived. She is still alive and speaking to schoolchildren in Berlin.

At the Zionskirche, on the border of Prenzlauer Berg and Mitte, Dietrich Bonhoeffer became the Protestant vicar in 1931 at the age of 25. He is well known for his resistance to the Nazis, along with his brother-in-law Hans von Dohnányi – a Reich Justice Ministry official who successfully rescued

German Jews and brought them to Switzerland. Dohnányi failed to assassinate Hitler in 1943. Both men were arrested and killed in camps on Hitler's orders in April 1945, just weeks before the war ended. Dohnányi said that he was simply 'on the path that a decent person inevitably takes'. But civil disobedience in wartime Berlin was more the exception than the rule. Another high-profile act of resistance was, of course, the July 1944 plot, when Nazi officers tried to assassinate Hitler; they are remembered in the Bendlerblock south of Tiergarten.

The final moments of the war for the Nazi leadership were played out close to the Brandenburg Gate in central Berlin. Hitler's bunker was the most fortified place in Germany, 10 metres underground, and reinforced with concrete, granite and steel, guarded by SS officers. It was built in two iterations by the firm Hochtief on the orders of the architect Albert Speer: the 1936 bunker was improved in 1944 as the capacity of bombs improved over the course of the Second World War. It took ages to destroy, the Soviets only half managing the job directly after the war, with the East Germans completing it in the 1980s.

The atmosphere here during the war was absurd and macabre, and would be mythically so if it were not part of history. Hitler had sealed himself not just physically but mentally from the realities outside, and never visited a bomb site. Goebbels read to him from the annals of Prussian history and his astrological cards, while Hitler, growing decrepit and weak – receiving amphetamine injections from his doctor and using cocaine eye drops – had childish temper tantrums. In the sprawling damp, sunless, unhealthy space, Hitler gave his Nero Decree on 19 March 1945, according to which Germany deserved only a total defeat – a decision that meant that Berlin would be taken and destroyed by the enemy, in a fanatical no-surrender. Throughout April, the situation deteriorated, and on 21 April the Soviets crossed the Berlin city limits. Hitler's advisors no longer stood up when he walked into the room, but remarkably Hitler remained in control. It was only on 30 April, after their infamous 31-hour marriage, that Hitler and Eva Braun committed double suicide. Their

Reichstag, Battle of Berlin, May 1945.

THE RED ARMY AND RAPE

Marta Hillers, a journalist who wrote an anonymous diary during the weeks of capitulation, recorded the experience of women who were treated as spoils of war by the Soviets, and then as damaged goods by those German men who returned from the front. Soviet soldiers, denied periods of rest and relaxation, and astonished to find Germans relatively well fed as they crossed into the Reich, looted not only food, radios and watches (in the famous victory photograph, the Soviet soldier hoisting the hammer and sickle above the Reichstag reportedly had a second watch on his arm airbrushed away by the censors). More than 100,000 women in Berlin were raped as reported by hospitals, but this is a conservative estimate. What is terrifying too is how inured German woman would become to this horrific violence. As Hillers wrote:

> What does it mean – rape? When I said the word for the first time aloud, Friday evening in the basement, it sent shivers down my spine. Now I can think it and write it with an untrembling hand, say it out loud to get used to hearing it said. It sounds like the absolute worst, the end of everything – but it's not.

Hillers's diary slipped into obscurity after the war – commentators at the time said it sullied the honour of German women – until *A Woman in Berlin*'s republication two years after the author's death in 2003, and popularization by the film version *Anonyma* in 2008. The recognition of rape as a crime against humanity in 2001, in a Hague Tribunal ruling regarding the Bosnian conflict of 1992–5, was just one indication of society's changing willingness to engage with a difficult subject.

A relief commemorating the Soviet victory in Berlin: Red Army soldiers are greeted by women with flowers. Soviet Memorial at Treptower Park (1949).

bodies were incinerated above ground in a location that is now a car park, overlooked by prefabricated East German modular state housing (*Plattenbau*), where the grand red-marble New Chancellery once stood. The state has not memorialized this site in any way.

The battle as experienced by ordinary Berliners was, needless to say, horrific. They suffered air raids (65,000 tons of bombs) and shelling (40,000 tons of shells). The sounds of the groaning artillery came to be known as 'Stalin's Organs'. The Nazi scorched-earth policy affected Berliners more than the invading Russians, who had their own supply lines. The Waffen SS's destruction in late April of Karstadt on Hermannplatz, one of Europe's largest department stores, and of food depots, are famous examples, and led to food riots and widespread looting. The atmosphere in the city was one of *Untergang*, or 'downfall', a 'desire to dispense with innocence': desperate hedonism, with sex in public places, and in the many bunkers and flak towers in which the civilian population cowered. Meanwhile, the very young (under sixteen) and old men (over fifty) who had up until now escaped uniform were forced into the city defences, the *Volkssturm*, blurring the line between combatant and civilian. Men were dragged out of hospitals; their uniforms did not fit; they did not know how to use a gun if they had one; 'tank' divisions proved to be squads of bicycles. Deserters, meanwhile, were shot and hanged from lamp posts pasted with signs reading: 'I am a coward', 'I am a traitor'. War happened street by street, inexorably, and at the last concert of the Berlin Philharmonic the Hitler Youth distributed cyanide capsules. Thousands committed suicide, and 150,000 fled the city west towards the advancing Americans in order not to fall into the hands of the Soviets, whose reputation for looting and mass rape preceded them.

Women of all ages who survived the siege of Berlin were then reduced to hard labour, as *Trümmerfrauen* ('rubble women') clearing roads and bomb sites. In the battle alone, 305,000 Soviets had died, and one million German troops. One hundred thousand civilians were killed. A quarter of the city was completely destroyed, rendering large sections unrecognizable, full of craters, corpses, rats, flies and stench, with no safe drinking water and trees cut down for fuel. More than half a million apartments were destroyed, making 1.5 million homeless, and the pre-war population was reduced by half, to 2.3 million.

On 2 May, when the city finally capitulated, the capital – which had enjoyed such a remarkable evolution from a small ford in a river to continental Europe's largest metropolis – was in such desperate ruins that some commentators were tempted to say that Germany, and Berlin, had experienced its 'zero hour'. But German history did not start afresh: longer themes would connect the post-war period to what had occurred before.

The Amerika Haus (now the C/O gallery), built in 1956–7 in West Berlin.

7 Division, and West Berlin (1945–1989)

The Americans arrived during the first days of July 1945. The great powers had already decided to divide the country into multiple zones. The division would eventually become a containment strategy to solve the historical 'German Question', to break into more manageable bits this troublesome state that was too powerful for its neighbours and deemed militaristic by nature, proved by its bellicosity in two world wars. As the joke later went, the world loved Germany so much it wanted more than one of her.

The Soviet Zone would occupy the East, the territory from the Elbe river to the Oder. Areas east of the Oder and Neisse rivers, or one-third of Germany's territory, would be annexed by other countries, in particular Poland and the Soviet Union. Berlin, once in the middle of Germany, would hug its new eastern border. More than twelve million German expellees, or *Vertriebene*, would lose their homes and be sent impoverished as refugees into rump Germany, a transfer that resulted in hundreds of thousands of deaths. Meanwhile, the western half would be divided between the British and American Zones, with a small section given to the French to restore their position among the Allies despite the fact that they had quickly surrendered to the Nazi advance.

To mirror the country as a whole, Berlin would also be divided. Each of the great powers took a number of districts. The division happened along the old borough lines established by the 1920 Greater Berlin Act. Eastern neighbourhoods, such as Mitte, Prenzlauer Berg, Friedrichshain, Treptow and Pankow, would go to the Soviets. Charlottenburg, Wilmersdorf and Spandau in the west went to the British. Schöneberg,

Kreuzberg, Neukölln, Tempelhof and the wealthy southwestern suburban areas of Berlin went to the Americans. The north (Reinickendorf and Wedding) went to the French. Because the Soviet Zone continued beyond the city limits, this meant that the western zones were surrounded by areas of Soviet control. Eventually, to reach West Germany from West Berlin, one would be forced to travel via one of three air corridors, or by land via a controlled transit route, either by rail or car. The Inner German border between West and East Germany was eventually more than 150 km from West Berlin.

The Potsdam Conference, which occurred from 17 July to 2 August 1945, shortly before the Americans set off nuclear bombs over Japanese cities, wedded the Allies to a plan of the 'three D's' – democratization, demilitarization and denazification – for the new Germany. But what the Soviets and Western Allies intended by these categories was not the same. In the Soviet Zone, democratization allowed for the existence of numerous political parties, but they were all made subservient to a Socialist Unity Party (or SED), which was the forced union in 1946 of the SPD and KPD. Meanwhile, large properties and businesses were collectivized. Demilitarization accompanied deindustrialization: the carrying away of 90 per cent of industry from the Eastern Zone by 1947. Denazification took the form of the conversion of former Nazi concentration camps, such as Sachsenhausen and Buchenwald, into detainment camps for those accused of anti-Soviet activities (a broad category). Of the 150,000 detained, 43,000 Germans died mostly from starvation in such 'Silence Camps' (named for their policy of total isolation). Meanwhile, in the Soviet Union, three million Germans were held as prisoners of war, and a third of them died.

In the Western Zones, the 'three D's' took a different course. There were multi-party democratic elections. Demilitarization did not accompany the war reparations demanded by the Soviets. The Americans, instead, anxious to create markets and not repeat the mistakes of the Versailles Peace, responded with a massive loan in the form of the Marshall Plan of 1947. Another locus of dispute with the Soviets was denazification. Despite the Nuremberg trials of 1945–6, which targeted a few high-ranking officials, the Western Zone, in the interest of quickly rebuilding the State bureaucracy, rehabilitated Nazis into structures as important as the police, secret service and government. By 1950, 60 per cent of civil servants in Bavaria were former party members. It would be an enduring criticism of the East towards the West that the latter had never properly denazified, and that capitalism remained the inheritor of the Nazi experience. This tension would be intensified in the divided capital.

A joint Allied Kommandatura governed the entire city from 11 July 1945 to 16 June 1948, and its breakdown was a symptom of the new Cold War. It might be a small footnote, but it is interesting to add that on 25 February 1947 the state of Prussia was formally abolished – that historic land of which Berlin had so long been the capital – because it was seen as the kernel of the 'German Question'. In 1949 two new states were declared that did not recognize one another: the German Democratic Republic in the East and the Federal Republic of Germany in the West. The former had its capital in Berlin, the latter in Bonn. In 1961 a wall separating the zones of occupied Berlin became a physical and psychological fact, symbolizing the division of Europe as a whole.

West Berlin, in the immediate post-Second World War period, found itself in a dreadful situation: 44,000 people still lived in emergency housing into the 1950s and one-quarter were unemployed. Berlin was, like other cities, brimming with refugees from the East. With the city in impoverished circumstances, the Soviets surrounding West Berlin cut off the supply lines, and from June 1948 until May 1949 the West flew in almost 1.5 million tons of supplies, on an airlift of more than 200,000 flights. Every two to three minutes an aeroplane heavy with goods landed to keep the Western Zone alive. The 'Berlin Blockade' was overcome, and in the process the old enemy West Berliners came to be seen as new allies of the Americans in a nascent Cold War.

The Konrad Adenauer government ruled West Germany from 1949 to 1963, overseeing the economic miracle, or

CANDY FROM THE SKY

Many children in West Berlin remember the blockade because of the 'raisin bombers' (*Rosinenbomber*). U.S. pilots would quiver their plane wings as a signal that they were releasing chocolate and sweets on small parachutes, and children would rush to grab them on the ground – young boys elbowing the girls out of the way. The story was sensationalized by the press, and kids in America raised money to buy Hershey's bars for West Berlin. By the end of the blockade, a stunning 22 tons of candy had been dropped over the city. The pilot originally responsible for the sensation, Gail Halvorsen, later described first dropping sweets from his C54:

> My copilot and engineer gave me their candy rations – big double handfuls of Hershey, Mounds and Baby Ruth bars, and Wrigley's gum. It was heavy, and I thought, 'Boy, put that in a bundle and hit 'em in the head going 100 miles an hour, it'll make the wrong impression.' So, I made three handkerchief parachutes and tied strings tight around the candy.
>
> The next day, I came in over the field, and there were those kids in that open space. I wiggled the wings, and they just blew up – I can still see their arms. The crew chief threw the rolled-up parachutes out the flare chute behind the pilot seat. Couldn't see what happened, of course . . . I worried all the time where the candy went. As we taxied out to takeoff, there were the kids, lined up on the barbed-wire fence, three handkerchiefs waving, their mouths going up and down like crazy.
>
> Three weeks we did it – three parachutes each time. The crowd got big.

Berlin children play the 'Berlin airlift' game in 1948.

Wirtschaftswunder, which increased West German purchasing power by 75 per cent in just a decade. The boom brought a labour shortage, and West Germany signed accords with countries like Italy and Yugoslavia to import 'guestworkers', seen at the time as a temporary source of labour. The influx of foreign workers meant big changes to the Berlin workforce, with many Germans switching from blue- to white-collar jobs, intensifying the perception of Germans as wealthy and immigrants as poor. With the Oil Crisis of the 1970s, and rising unemployment, immigrants – who had been expected to return 'home' – came ultimately to be seen by many as an economic drain. In the meantime, they had not been provided with sufficient German-language or integration skills. This was a swift reversal for a population previously seen as necessary for post-war reconstruction.

The 1961 treaty with Turkey would have the most enduring impact on the city of Berlin, as families joined to constitute the immigrant heart of neighbourhoods such as Kreuzberg and Wedding. They would face accompanying problems of economic disenfranchisement and racism. Berlin today has half a million residents who are not German citizens; the population with a 'migration' background (with citizenship) is 25 per cent, of which 200,000 originated in Turkey. The immigration wave of 2015 added significantly to the numbers from Syria and Afghanistan.

The West Berlin which developed was an 'island in the red sea' of East Germany, especially once the Berlin Wall was built around it. Although it became famous on the front line of the Cold War, its status as a 'Great City' was clearly diminished. The writer Kerstin Schilling explained,

> The word 'metropolis' indeed never really fitted West Berlin . . . The half-city was too immobile, too fixed, too slow, even though more daring when comparing, for example, its music scene of the 80s with other cities. And yet . . . we realized that in this narrowness and seclusion we felt very much at home.

But West Berlin, although provincial, was very unusual. The Berlin allowance (*Berlinzulage* or *Zitterprämie*, 'jitters premium') was an 8 per cent tax-free wage bonus, to encourage residence in a territory under threat. Berlin was highly subsidized, privileged, a showcase of the West, with a proliferation of projects intended to boast the achievements of Western modern architecture, such as Hugh Stubbins's 'pregnant oyster', the House of World Cultures, of 1957; the *Interbau 1957* projects of Alvar Aalto, Arne Jacobsen, Oscar Niemeyer and others in the Hansaviertel; and Hans Scharoun's 'Karajan circus' at the Philharmonic Hall in 1963.

Counterculture flourished here. The high number of universities and schools, and the fact that one was exempt from military service in West Berlin, added to the number of anti-authoritarian young people. Violence against student leaders and demonstrators in the late 1960s was followed by a spate of home-grown terrorism in the 1970s. The student leader Rudi Dutschke, a high-profile figure from the era,

The Berlin Philharmonic Hall.

survived an assassination attempt in 1968 (he died a decade later from his injuries). And Benno Ohnesorg, when participating in his first-ever demonstration on 2 June 1967 outside the Deutsche Oper against the state visit of the Shah of Iran, was shot by a West Berlin police officer, Karl-Heinz Kurras (the latter turned out to be an agent of the East German Stasi – a murky story with still unanswered questions). The death of Ohnesorg became a symbol of the continued brutality of the German State towards militants. This State violence was seen by many as a continuity of the Nazi period, expressing a piquant form of generational conflict.

Gudrun Ensslin, a leader of the Red Army Faction, the core of 1970s violent militarism, proclaimed, 'This fascist state means to kill us all. We must organize resistance. Violence is the only way to answer violence. This is the Auschwitz Generation, and there is no arguing with them!' West German politics had, however, on the whole taken a leftward turn with the election of the former mayor of Berlin, Willy Brandt, as Chancellor. He brought about successful negotiations with East Germany, with his *Ostpolitik*, and mutual recognition between the divided halves in 1972.

Other aspects of Berlin's rebellion included the music scene, the Vietnam protests and the *Haschrebellen*, who called themselves, in their war for drug freedom, the 'militant heart of Berlin subculture'. There have been divergent evaluations of so much protest in such a wealthy and privileged place as West Berlin. As the poet Ingeborg Bachmann wryly put it, 'The new religion comes from Kreuzberg, the holy beards and commands, the revolution against the subsidized death throes.' Others point to the darker face of the drug scene in West Berlin, seen in the taped confessionals of a teenager, Christiane F., who at thirteen was coerced into the violent drug and sex trade around the Zoologischer Garten Station. But for many, West Berlin offered an important example for those who promoted alternative living, be it in the squat movement that proliferated in the 1980s, or through rising federal political forces such as the Green Party. And of course not all West Berlin was 'alternative', any more than it is today

– the luxury mile of Kurfürstendamm, or *Ku'damm*, one of the first areas to be refurbished after the war, was the epitome of the consumerist decadence against which so much of the counterculture was reacting.

In late 1976 a young Englishman of 29 named David Bowie, newly famous on the glam rock scene, arrived in Berlin. He lived in Schöneberg, at Hauptstrasse 155, and frequented the little café downstairs called Neues Ufer. In the city, he recorded three albums now known as his 'Berlin Trilogy', including *Heroes* (1977), in the Hansa Studios, collaborating with Brian Eno and sharing his flat with Iggy Pop. Bowie said later that one of his reasons for moving to Berlin was to escape the 'drug-induced calamity' of his life in Los Angeles. He was also apparently inspired by German Expressionists and the West German electronic pioneers Kraftwerk. But, similar to so many young artists coming to Berlin today, he found that

> For many years, Berlin had appealed to me as a sort of sanctuary-like situation. It was one of the few cities where I could move around in virtual anonymity. I was going broke; it was cheap to live. For some reason, Berliners just didn't care. Well, not about an English rock singer anyway.

He experienced a little of what is called *Berliner Wurschtigkeit*; what other people get up to is not interesting, it's all just *Wurscht* (or 'sausage'). Bowie came to Berlin to disappear, to seek out that seclusion and quietness one needs in order to create. As he said in 2001, Berlin was 'a city that's so easy to "get lost" in – and to "find" oneself too'. The devastated, island world of the West provided just the right amount of alienation – but also a flicker of protest.

8 East Berlin (1945–1989)

Imagine you are walking through Prenzlauer Berg in the 1980s. There is the feeling of a country that has never recovered from war and is, in fact, more economically depressed and in worse repair than in any period since the beginning of the century. The facades are crusted with coal; an old lady was killed by a falling balcony just the other week. The air smells like a mix of gas and oil, the two-stroke engine of the Trabant car, and of soft coal, which is how you heat your home. The air is polluted, like many places in the country. It is a society in uniform, or working very resourcefully to look different: leather jackets, tight white pants. There's little advertising. The bakery down the street makes what it can; they're collecting raisins in the summer so they have enough for the Christmas *Stollen*. There are places at the end of the street, where you cannot go, just around the corner from here, at the end of Bernauer Strasse. From some buildings, you can just see over the Wall to West Berlin.

For many, the experience of the East was typified not by these daily sights and smells, but by the way protest met differing responses from those in the West. The State was engineered to control dissent, both through armed action and unprecedented surveillance. On 17 June 1953 Soviet troops put down an embarrassing workers' uprising. The workers were protesting against low pay and conditions on mass construction projects, such as the avenue of socialist-Classical architecture on Stalinallee (today's Karl-Marx-Allee). Eventually SED buildings elsewhere went up in flames, with thousands protesting before the former Nazi Air Force Ministry, which had become the House of East German

The bureaucracy behind a Stasi prison, in the Gedenkstätte Berlin-Hohenschönhausen (Berlin-Hohenschönhausen Memorial).

Ministries, site of the signing of the East German constitution in 1949. The Soviet government reacted with tremendous force: 28,000 soldiers and police were deployed, and hundreds of people were killed or injured. Half a million Soviet soldiers would remain in the GDR at any one time, with ten million deployed over the almost fifty years of occupation, normally without contact with the local population, unlike the Americans, who fraternized freely with Germans.

A portion of the social time of East German citizens was organized: that of children, for example, in the pioneer-style programme the Free German Youth (Freie Deutsche Jugend, of which 75 per cent of all 14-to-25-year-olds were members). But the remaining private space was also controlled from 1950 through another agency, the 'shield and sword' of the party, the Stasi (*Staatssicherheit*) or State Security Service. The head of the agency from 1957 to 1989, Erich Mielke, was a former assassin involved in a 1931 double homicide. In a strange twist of East German sports history (with its notorious dopings and youth camps), Mielke was a puppeteer of East German football teams, promoting his Berlin Stasi team, BFC Dynamo, which, through his enormous, conniving influence, became East Germany's best.

The Stasi was a system of 'official' and 'unofficial' informants. The unofficials, *Inoffizielle Mitarbeiter* or IMs, reportedly accounted for one-eighth of the population, with ten thousand of them under the age of eighteen. The remarkable amount of reporting, or files, finally became available to East German citizens after reunification, revealing the extent to which their private lives had been observed by neighbours or even lovers ('Romeos' who had been assigned to obtain information through intimacy). Individuals were tracked through smell samples, tapped rooms and phone lines. Those detained endured new forms of torture, such as deliberate exposure to radiation. Mountains of files, more than 600 million pages, were shredded (and then torn by hand when the shredders broke) by the authorities in the rush of the fall of the Berlin Wall. These files constitute the world's largest jigsaw puzzle and have been, and continue to be, painstakingly put back together, first by individuals employed by the federal government, and increasingly by the 'ePuzzler', which digitizes and reconstructs the ripped pages. As a result, new information continually emerges about the Stasi's pervasive authority in the East German regime. No regime had ever in history so thoroughly invaded personal privacy violations – the Stasi were only outdone in the twenty-first century, with the development of online surveillance. Germany continues to have an extremely critical approach, both legally and in public attitudes, to Internet privacy violations, making Berlin the centre of the world's encryption and whistle-blower community. Public concern with privacy is no doubt intensified because of the long shadow of the Stasi and the Gestapo.

The final, most famous instrument of control in the East was of course the Berlin Wall, built in 1961. In the late 1950s Berlin was in the front line of an international crisis. The Soviets, worried about the potential nuclear arming of West Germany, demanded a 'Free City'. And while Walter Ulbricht, the first General Secretary of the SED, said on 15 June 1961 that 'no one has the intention of building a wall', a wall was finally the Soviet response. Because it promoted détente, the Berlin Wall was in fact welcomed (although not officially) by President John F. Kennedy, who would soon enough negotiate America through the Cuban Missile Crisis of 1962. But for Berliners the Wall was a tragedy. Between spring 1949 and August 1961, three million East Germans left for the West, and the Wall was built in part to prevent more from leaving.

It went up overnight on 13 August 1961 – first as a perimeter of guarded barbed wire and building structures encircling the western neighbourhoods – on a Sunday, when people were not expected to be at work. Until the Wall was built, 52,000 Easterners had been allowed to travel daily to the West to work. Comings and goings were imperfectly controlled, as one can see in the film *One, Two, Three* (dir. Billy Wilder, 1961). There were several iterations of the Wall that followed, and it became a sophisticated structure of an interior and exterior wall, with ditches, tank traps, patrol towers, guard dogs and an alarm fence. The combed sand of the death strip, where footsteps were easily visible, was the most dangerous space of the Wall complex.

One remarkable location was Bernauer Strasse, where the buildings were in the East but the pavement was in the West.

A Socialist mural from 1952, located at the current Ministry of Finance, or former House of the Ministries.

Cyclists cross Strausberger Platz, a showpiece of Communist-era construction along Karl-Marx-Allee. It was one of the locations where vigorous workers' protests occurred on 17 June 1953.

It became a loophole in those first days after the Wall's construction, where you could literally jump from your kitchen window to freedom. Another anomaly of the site was that an 1894 church (appropriately named the Chapel of Reconciliation) was trapped in no-man's land and left standing until it was detonated by the GDR in 1985. On its site today is a mud brick and clay structure that contains the rubble of the previous church. The buildings on Bernauer Strasse, with their windows bricked up, eventually became the Wall itself. The State's memorial to the Berlin Wall on Bernauer Strasse (not at Checkpoint Charlie, which is a private venture) – complete with inner and outer walls and death strip – can be seen from the roof of the Gedankstätte Museum.

There were many iconic escapes at Bernauer Strasse after the Wall was built, including that of Conrad Schumann, the nineteen-year-old border guard who defected while on duty on 15 August 1961, and the tunnel diggers who allowed 57 people to escape through a 145-metre passage from a basement in Mitte across to Wedding on 3–4 October 1964. Forty thousand people escaped altogether, including 2,500 border guards. At least 136 people, meanwhile, died in the Wall area, including eight border guards. One of the first victims of the Wall was a 58-year-old woman, Ida Siekmann, who on 22 August jumped from a building on Bernauer Strasse. Another well-known victim was the eighteen-year-old Peter Fechter who, on 17 August 1962, bled to death in the border strip, left alone, as Western media filmed him. One of the last victims would be a young waiter working in the restaurant of the East German airport Schönefeld, Chris Gueffroy, 21 years old, who had heard that the border police had stopped firing on escapees. He had been misinformed, and, trying to get across the canal between Treptow and Neukölln on 5 February 1989, he was shot through the heart.

The Berlin Wall became the symbol of the Cold War itself. It represented one of the strangest sociological experiments ever undertaken: taking one people joined by a long history, dividing them under two ideological systems, and then, more than two generations later, putting them back together. The Berlin Wall divided Germany: in the East, it was called the 'anti-fascist protection wall', and in the West it proved the Communist system's inhumanity. But it was also the single greatest argument that the two Germanies belonged together, simply because they needed to be kept apart. The Wall is therefore sometimes called 'the zip', because it both connected and separated the two Germanies.

Film culture in the GDR is revealing of themes in East German society often overlooked by political historians. A 1957 film, *Berlin, Schönhauser Corner*, directed by Gerhard Klein, like Christa Wolf's *Divided Heaven* (1963) treats the emigration theme, but in the period before the Berlin Wall. It too looked to Western styles, a kind of East German *Rebel Without a Cause*, with delinquent greasers. Hanging out under the tracks of the U2 Dimitroffstrasse (now Eberswalder Strasse) stop, in Prenzlauer Berg, they soon discover that true criminality, in the guise of murder, comes from the West. Konrad Wolf's film *Solo Sunny* (1980) is another that shows the infiltration of Western influences into East German society, this time in terms of the cult of rock 'n' roll stardom. It is an atmospheric story of a young woman making it big in the East German music industry, a compelling and paradoxical narrative about individual ambition in a collective system.

But if one film produced by DEFA, the State-owned film studio, were to stand in for the experience of a generation of East Berliners, it must be Heiner Carow's *The Legend of Paul and Paula* (1973) and its *Ostrock* soundtrack by the Brandenburg band Pudhys. The story of Paul, who has an affair with single mother Paula, has none of the expected moral disapproval of infidelity, although the fate of the couple is tragic. The film was as unpopular with the authorities as it was popular with the public, for its frank depictions of sexuality, emphasis on individual pleasure, careful ironizing of Stasi agents and critical view on the destruction of Berlin's old neighbourhoods to make room for mass housing projects. Only the intervention of the Communist General Secretary Erich Honecker, who appreciated the need for East German cinema to appeal to younger audiences, kept the film in cinemas.

Vintage Trabants. The 'Trabis', as the cars are affectionately called, were manufactured between 1957 and 1990.

The World Clock in Alexanderplatz.

After reunification, *The Legend of Paul and Paula* remained a major cult classic and source of *Ostalgie* (nostalgia for the East) – despite the fact that it was popular in the 1970s precisely because it challenged the authorities. And yet the popularity of the film also reveals something that many of the post-1989 histories of East Germany, focusing on the brutality of the Stasi or on the Wall, leave out: the fact that East Germany was a country with its own youth culture – film, art and music scene – to which many had tied their collective experiences of (an often very happy) upbringing, in a country that was richer than its Eastern neighbours. Many felt that these memories, and the ideal of a better social reality, were invalidated with the scrapping of East Germany, and the subsequent critical reception of its history. Accompanying the zeitgeist of *Ostalgie* was disapproval of the former West Germany's lack of self-criticism regarding the failures of its own ideological system, capitalism. The focus on politics also left out, for many, what nonetheless, and inexorably, continued regardless of oppression – the joys and intimacies of private and family life – reducing an era to: 'things in East Germany were mostly bad, and a little bit good.'

The 2015 production of Christa Wolf's *Divided Heaven* at the Schaubühne Theatre, directed by Armin Petras.

CHRISTA WOLF'S *DIVIDED HEAVEN*

The Wall intensified the imagination surrounding escape from the East. It is intriguing to reflect on the work of the novelist Christa Wolf who, writing shortly after the building of the Berlin Wall, tells the story of why one might choose to stay in the East rather than emigrate to the West. Wolf is accused of writing propaganda, and later it became clear that she briefly worked for the Stasi; but her love story, *Divided Heaven*, of a couple, Rita and Manfred, who find themselves separated by emigration over the barrier, is poignant. When Rita visits Manfred, finally, in West Berlin right before the Wall is built, the latter lives in a world of garish advertisements and wilted trees, while Rita looks idealistically to the sky, where the promise of Socialism's triumph, in the form of sputnik, is rising. 'You cannot divide the sky,' says Manfred, but she is not so sure. *Divided Heaven* was beautifully adapted to film in 1964, in the style of the French New Wave, by the director Konrad Wolf, who had fled to the Soviet Union as a young boy when the Nazis came to power, joined the Red Army and participated in the Battle of Berlin. Not always popular with the regime because of its discussion of emigration to the West, the film was one of the most popular ever produced by the East German production company DEFA.

9 The Turning Point (1989–1991)

Pipes reconnected, subway lines re-joined, the island of West Berlin would soon find itself reopened to its hinterland. One of the great failures of political science has been its inability to predict the fall of the Berlin Wall on 9 November 1989, used as shorthand to mean the fall of the Communist system everywhere in the East. As the Soviet Union imploded, the satellite states in Central Europe were able to relax their grip on their citizens. The resulting (dramatic, sudden and imperfect) reunification happened at a dizzying speed. Berliners, who had already found themselves in the strange experiment of one city with two systems, now found societies that had grown very far apart stitched back together.

Although at the highest levels of government there was instability, with Erich Honecker recovering from bladder cancer, the State was nonetheless planning a shambolic fortieth anniversary celebration of the GDR on 7 October 1989. The Soviet Union was the real fountainhead of change, because of internal economic and political strife, which spread from the centre. The USSR was overstretched militarily, signalled by its withdrawal from Afghanistan in February. Gorbachev's policies of glasnost and perestroika had changed conditions radically in Moscow, and by 1989 it was clear that the USSR would no longer enforce the Brezhnev Doctrine (the 1968 affirmation that the Soviet Union would invade to protect state socialism behind the Iron Curtain).

This presented an opportunity for the more renegade of the Iron Curtain nations. Hungary had always been the most daring of the Eastern states, along with Poland, where the dock workers of the Solidarity movement had initiated a mass uprising in 1980–81. On 2 May Hungary, after having relaxed its visa regime, rolled up its barbed-wire fence with Austria, creating the first gap in the Iron Curtain. This meant that East Germans, permitted to holiday behind it, could slip across the border. A quarter of a million East Germans were holidaying in Hungary in August 1989, and 25,000 of them left for the West in those weeks. Soon enough, the Czechs opened their borders, and, seeing this on contraband West German television, widely available in the East, other East Germans followed. Meanwhile, West Germans hopefully but nervously watched the developing refugee crisis, which was reuniting the German population on West German soil.

A more challenging problem faced East Germany: how to respond to the departures, whether to place the entire country under house arrest, and how to react to the Monday demonstrations in Leipzig, which had been intensifying and spreading to other cities since early September. A draconian precedent had been provided in early June that year when the Chinese killed protestors at Tiananmen Square. The GDR regime, however, followed the lead of its neighbours when it developed a new travel bill. On 9 November, a Politburo member, Günter Schabowski, casually announced at its press conference that the requirement to have a visa to leave the GDR had been lifted with immediate effect. He went far beyond what the Politburo had agreed, but his words had already been broadcast across the Germanies by West German television.

East German citizens rushed to the Wall and hoped to be let through on the night of 9 November 1989. One border crossing was at Bornholmer Strasse, between the French and Soviet Zones, where crowds pushed to cross a bridge where the frontier ran along the rail lines. There was a moment of hesitation. Would the border guards fire? Would they let through the crowds?

The border guards were faced with an overwhelming situation and telephoned for instructions from superiors, who, in a state of chaos, would not issue specific orders. The news conference had surprised those responsible for the checkpoints as much as the public. Lieutenant-Colonel

The Bornholmer Strasse memorial to the Berlin Wall. In the foreground is the memorial, in the background the Berlin Wall itself.

Harald Jäger, responsible at Bornholmer Strasse, was later interviewed by *Der Spiegel*. Faced with the demanding crowd of thousands outside, he assembled his officers and asked them what to do:

> *Jäger*: I said: 'Should I let the GDR citizens leave? Or should I give the order to open fire?' 'For God's sake!' they said. I only mentioned opening fire as a provocation [Jäger claims this was never an option]; I wanted to know if they would support me if I allowed the GDR citizens to cross over. It was clear that it would be my responsibility but I wanted to be sure I would have their support. But that wasn't forthcoming. That's how the meeting ended . . . People could have been injured or killed even without shots being fired. In scuffles, or if there had been panic among the thousands gathered at the border crossing. That's why I gave my people the order: Open the barrier!

Shortly before midnight, the first who crossed had their passports invalidated, but soon the crowd overwhelmed the stunned guards. All this happened first at Bornholmer Strasse,

The Reichstag dome, refurbished by Sir Norman Foster.

then elsewhere in Berlin. Soon enough people were dancing on top of the Wall that had separated families and were freely breaching the deadly spaces between the two sides of the structure where many had died.

At first, there was the possibility that the GDR might remain its own country. But with free elections in March, East Germans voted for the Christian Democrats (CDU), as a gesture of support for the ruling sister party in West Germany and Chancellor Helmut Kohl. The vote also represented approval of the CDU's intent to fast-track transition and quickly bring hard currency to the people of the East (who by now, with free movement, had an even better idea of the consumables citizens in the West had that they did not). On 1 July 1990 currency union also meant that East German marks could be converted one to one up to a total of 4,000.

The West German government, taking the opportunity of the chaos accompanying the unfolding dissolution of the Soviet Union, and after many tense negotiations with Western powers nervous about the re-emergence of the 'German Question', pursued political union to follow on economic union. This occurred on 3 October 1990, with the establishment of five new German *Länder*, or states.

IN THE
to: MiRCO and
DONA

The fall of the Wall, November 1989.

My First Banana', from the satirical magazine *Titanic* (November 1989). Many East Berliners had never tried this fruit before the Wall fell

WELCOME MONEY

East Germans arriving in the West were given 100 DM of *Begrüssungsgeld*, or 'welcome money'. How individuals spent their 'welcome money' makes for good conversation with Berliners. Some bought pornography or drugs, which were highly regulated in the East; others went to KaDeWe to buy an appliance; others simply saved the funds. Tropical fruit, espresso coffee, shop-bought strawberries, fine chocolate and French wine were just some of the products of which Easterners had little experience. These new consumers would have been surprised to know that, only a few years later, Eastern products, formerly derided – such as Mocha-Fix Gold Coffee, Tempo beans and Spreewald pickles – would gain cult status, made famous internationally by the film *Good Bye Lenin!* (2003). An archetypal *Ossi* purchase during *Die Wende* was the banana, a fruit rare in the East. This stereotypical trope had already been seized on by the *Wessi* satirical magazine *Titanic*, for their November 1989 issue, 'My First Banana'. An *Ossi* woman (known as 'Zonen-Gaby'), with a short perm and in a denim shirt, holds a cucumber peeled like a banana. Many West Berliners laughed rather too easily, disparagingly, at the poverty of East Berliners and their unfamiliarity with consumer choice. Meanwhile, East Berliners were overwhelmed by Western consumerism and individualism, and what they perceived as accompanying crassness. The banana debate, of course, reduces the impact of 'welcome money' to superfluous expenditures. At a reception I once met an art historian couple from the former East who had studied French classical painting all their lives but had never been to the Louvre. They spent their welcome money on an overnight bus trip to Paris so that they could finally see the paintings they had studied for years but never been allowed to see in person.

The inhabitants of the German Democratic Republic bade their country goodbye.

It is extraordinary to think that it took only from 9 November 1989 to 3 October 1990 for a new country to be born, bringing two peoples together who for almost fifty years had followed separate developments under separate political systems. The basis for reunification was, of course, history and language, but also blood. The last time they had been together was during the Nazi period, when notions of blood and belonging had dominated political discussion. And yet, for most, the events of 1990 represented the triumph of freedom over the inhumanity of authoritarian control symbolized by the Berlin Wall; the dismantling of a system that had perverted the promises of socialism; and the end of the hovering nuclear threat that had hung over Berlin as the front line between the superpowers.

One of the most unusual reflections on this period must be the 2009 documentary *Mauerhase* (or *Rabbit à la Berlin*, dir. Bartosz Konopka) that presents, with its tongue in its cheek, the Berlin Wall from the perspective of the rabbits who burrowed along the death strip, protected from predators by the Wall and its guards. They were shaded by the tank traps, nourished by one monotonous species of grass, and grew indolent in their giant, socialized zoo paradise looping Berlin. For them, the fall of the Wall was a tragedy. For Berliners, it would be a decidedly exceptional adventure – of stitching the city back together, or into something new.

10 The Berlin Renaissance (1991–Present)

Berlin in the 1990s became a legendary maze of abandoned industrial spaces, electronic sounds from empty buildings and the stark remaining differences between East and West. But it was also a place of mass unemployment and economic uncertainty. Reunification was achieved swiftly – this is the most stunning thing about it – but was it done well?

There were big plans for Berlin shortly after reunification, based on population projections that erroneously predicted that the city would grow by one million people in ten years. As part of the reunification treaty, the capital was moved back to Berlin in 1990, although certain ministries would remain in Bonn. Propelled by grand expectations for the new capital, Berlin became a city of cranes. The government centre saw the building of a whole new infrastructure, the former no-man's area of Potsdamer Platz became a corporate centre of undistinguished high-rises, and the state embarked on a number of high-profile memorial projects to prove that despite unification and its growing power it remained contrite for its past crimes.

But the relocation of the capital added only a hundred thousand government employees to Berlin. The idea of merging the state of Berlin with the state of Brandenburg, which would have resulted in a greater metropolitan area of almost six million, was defeated by referendum on 5 May 1996. Meanwhile in East Germany as a whole, the population shrank. Half a million people had left per year in 1989 and 1990, and the exodus remained over fifty thousand per year until 1993. Meanwhile, birth rates in the former East plummeted.

East Berlin's population between 1989 and 1995 remained essentially the same partly because in certain neighbourhoods there was population replacement: in Prenzlauer Berg, for example, 80 per cent of the population was replaced by young people arriving mostly from former West Germany to occupy cheap apartments. The prediction that the population of Berlin would grow by one million in ten years ultimately proved false, with a loss of fifty thousand people by the year 2000. (In the following years, 'P Berg' – with its markets of hand-made wooden toys, hordes of children descending on playgrounds, and the notorious demands of the 'mothers of Kollwitzplatz' ('Is that really organic?') – promised Europe's highest birth rate, but that too was more myth than reality.)

Berlin had been Germany's industrial capital before the Second World War. It remained so in the East during state socialism, but by 1990 the industry there was that of another generation. Unable to compete with the West, the Eastern factory belt along the Spree river, and other areas, were de-industrialized (making way for spectacular club spaces and squats, despite problems with hazardous industrial waste). Meanwhile, the controversial Treuhand agency, responsible for the selling and restitution of state-owned concerns in the East, oversaw restructuring and job loss. Between 1989 and 1993, manufacturing jobs fell by 75 per cent. East German workers fled to well-paying jobs in Bavaria and Baden-Württemberg. Meanwhile, unemployment rose to close to 20 per cent across Berlin by the end of the decade. These changes were a traumatic reversal for the erstwhile protected island of West Berlin, which had its subsidies scrapped.

In 2001 one of Germany's most high-profile banking scandals of the post-war period erupted in Berlin – a messy affair of corruption and property speculation – with a €30 billion bailout of the state-owned Berliner Bankgesellschaft. The CDU government fell in its wake, and SPD mayor Klaus Wowereit came to power. His reign would come to an end in 2014 owing to another scandal (the planned cost of the mismanaged Berlin-Brandenburg Airport tripled to almost €6 billion; it is now delayed by a half-decade, and will still be closed when this edition goes to press). The bank's failure in 2001 impoverished public finances in Berlin, bringing the deficit to €60 billion. This hardly made Berlin the prosperous capital of a resurgent Germany, as had been expected. Meanwhile, elsewhere in Germany, taxpayers were faced with post-unification buyer's remorse. Over twenty years €1.3 trillion of subsidies would be sunk into the East.

Such economic instability was also a shock to many in the East who were used to guaranteed housing and official full employment. These near-certainties were replaced with a number of welfare reforms, most recently the much debated Hartz IV programme. In the September 2016 Berlin state elections, Die Linke – the successor to the former East German Communist Party – won 15.6 per cent of the votes, enough to be partners in a coalition government. Most of their support came from the former Eastern neighbourhoods, on a platform prioritizing employment, welfare reform and guaranteed housing. Meanwhile it was the East that also voted for the xenophobic Alternative for Germany (AfD) party (14.2 per cent). Divisions between East and West have been slow to disappear. The Wall remained 'in people's heads' even when it

Berlin as a constant building site.

WOLFGANG TILLMANS

A German artist and winner of the Turner Prize in 2000, Wolfgang Tillmans (1968–), made his career in the UK and used to work between London and Berlin. But in 2014, he moved his gallery entirely to the German capital. His non-profit exhibition space, 'Between Bridges', is now located in Keithstrasse, close to Wittenbergplatz, while his working space is not far from Kottbusser Tor in Kreuzberg, occupying a floor of a former 1930s department store. Tillmans is something of a bellwether for London artists, and that a photographer of such international importance has departed is telling. 'London's not a write-off,' Tillmans told the *Berliner Morgenpost*, 'But it's going through a difficult period.' Even as old Berliners remark on just how much more expensive everything is becoming, new British arrivals, with fewer resources than Tillmans, continue to be wowed by Berlin's comparative affordability. Tillmans was attracted, however, by the city's non-corporate atmosphere: 'Berlin still has quite an edge because it lacks certain concepts of behavioural control that are at work in places like London or New York – how to be "it" for example.' He returns to Berlin famous, but in the early 1990s he was still trying to make his name in the city, photographing the Love Parade, Berlin's rave culture and the gay scene. This messy youth culture is captured with great luminosity. Perhaps the early Berlin works are so compelling because his grubby, sexy subjects contrast so surprisingly with the clarity of his photographic idiom, which is reminiscent of a seventeenth-century still-life.

Wolfgang Tillmans, *The Cock (kiss)*, 2002.

was physically removed, and many in the East feel they have been colonized by the West and that their country has been taken from them.

And with unification, what it meant to be German came into question. The costly reunification happened on the basis of history, ethnicity and language. Many immigrant communities in the West, including the Turkish and Arabic communities centred in Kreuzberg, Neukölln and Wedding, wondered whether they were also the 'people' in the project of nation-building. *Wir sind auch das Volk* was a response to the motto of unification, which was *Wir sind das Volk* ('We are the people'). A unification based on historical precedents, and ethnicity, which is what the 1990 unification was, implicitly challenged the role of immigrants in the country, who saw the association of blood with belonging as a spectre from Nazi times and before. In the West the influx of mostly Turkish guest workers had changed the face of German society, and on the other side, in the East, there was much less diversity. The shock of seeing difference when the Wall opened created misunderstandings, and, in those first years, in 1991 and 1992, there were racially motivated attacks in towns like Hoyerswerda and Rostock. Still today, there is statistically a very high level of racism in rural former East Germany (a problem, of course, not isolated to just the East, although the AfD has proved strongest in the former GDR).

The discussion of national belonging evolved in the early 2000s. Germans often refer to the 2006 football World Cup as the moment when they finally started to feel proud of their country again. This generated a tremendous public debate about flag-waving (flags had hitherto often been associated with the far right), and whether the united Germans had a right to pride. As one foreign correspondent wrote at the time,

> To say the World Cup has allowed Germany to love itself again would be overly simplistic: that process has been a long one at whose difficulties we can largely only guess. But witnessing the manic euphoria that broke out in Berlin's streets after the host nation beat Portugal on Saturday to

At the LAGeSo registration centre, thousands of new refugees faced agonizing waits of weeks or months (September 2015).

> be placed third in the tournament, it was hard not to feel an irresistible sea change has taken place in this country over the past five weeks.

The change in permissible levels of German pride is related to the slow disappearance of the Nazi generation directly responsible for German crimes. To have been an adult over eighteen in the last year of the war, one would have had had to have been 79 years old during the 2006 World Cup (or 90 years old in 2017). This has transformed the level of guilt young Germans feel about the past, and those who came from 'migration backgrounds' wondered why they should feel any guilt at all (if their grandparents spent the Second World War in, say, Turkey).

SOLDATEN SIND... MÖRDER!
STILL ♥ING LINKE TERRORNESTER
BESORGTEN „BÜRGERN" & NAZI-MOB
IHREM
DIE ZÄHNE ZIEHEN
IN HEIDENAU, NAUEN & ÜBERALL

The mass influx of war refugees and other migrants from the Middle East and North Africa in 2015 faced considerable resistance in former Eastern regions such as Saxony, where the anti-Islam party the AfD grew in popularity. In Berlin, however, the reaction was different: 75 per cent of Berliners, from former East and West, initially said they would welcome refugees when polled. Almost 80,000 arrived in the capital in 2015, following Chancellor Angela Merkel's open-door policy, but the state administration – overwhelmed by the numbers, inflexible in its procedures, incapable of coping with rapid change – was unable efficiently to register the new arrivals and provide services for them. By December human rights lawyers had sued LAGeSo (the Berlin State Office for Health and Social Affairs) for dangerous conditions, as refugees battled with security for entrance to the office or collapsed from hypothermia at its doorstep. Meanwhile, Berliners mobilized with grassroots social service projects in response to the historic migration, as their streets were visibly transformed by the presence of the new arrivals. But 2016 brought with it a series of high-profile Islamist terrorist attacks in Europe, and the public mood of inclusion began to shift. On 19 December 2016, a lorry plowed fatally through a Christmas Market in Berlin's Old West, raising questions about whether Berlin too would continue to be so welcoming.

As Germany rediscovered pride and its power, other expatriates rediscovered Berlin, and the capital became a byword for 'cool' and 'youth culture', attracting thousands of young artists and 'hipsters', many of them unemployed youth refugees from the very Eurozone economies languishing under austerity policies designed in the German capital. The creative vibrancy, especially in theatre, music and visual art, has been compared to the Weimar Republic years, hence the name 'the Berlin Renaissance'. With Berlin gentrifying, internationalizing

An occupied house, or squat, in Mitte.

The Kater Holzig club space, as it appeared in 2010. It has since been torn down to build luxury apartments.

and becoming increasingly forward-looking, many Berliners, however, feel the change has been too quick and would prefer the city to remain an exceptional island. Rising rents and living costs have been the bane of the half-million welfare recipients in the city. A number of recent films (*Berlin Calling*, *Oh Boy!*, *Victoria*) draw from Berlin 'cool' and express disenchantment. Sociologists debate whether tourists and artists have benefited from the poverty and unemployment of the city, or whether they coexist with it.

Berlin today, after the economic travails of the twenty years following reunification, is resurgent: busy, heavily touristed, with a booming property market and a proliferation of start-ups, despite financial troubles all over Europe and the challenge of refugee arrivals. It finds itself the capital of an optimistic, growing, export-driven and – to the consternation of some – politically bold Germany. In European economic policy, it has arguably become Europe's de facto capital (especially post-Brexit). These developments have been accompanied locally by the ills of gentrification that put pressure on Berlin's most vulnerable. Berlin's re-emergence as Europe's arts and youth capital has made it internationally famous, although this lustre is tarnished by its success, as it is 'discovered' and commercialized.

The term 'Renaissance' raises the question, of what? Should we read too much into the claim that this 'Renaissance' Berlin is a second 'Weimar', emerging from a revolution, recovering from economic troubles and now in its stabilization phase, facing demons of nationalistic overweening self-confidence? Should this not make us very wary of where it is going? Of course, the comparison is overly deterministic; history rhymes but it does not repeat. Luckily, neither Berlin today, nor Germany, is militaristic in character (although some say its economic policies are) or politically polarized. Democracy has deep, not shallow roots, and diversity is a fact of the city, not disputed territory to the extent it was in earlier centuries. Berlin is the capital of a country that, although it commemorates victims better than it exposes perpetrators, has examined its conscience and is inoculated against the far right – despite the AfD's gains

– more effectively than, say, many of its neighbours. The city, because it remains comparatively affordable, has attracted creative types from around the world, adding to a young population busy (or not) with university life.

Berlin remains in many ways provincial, an island, but one that is decidedly socially conscious and, still in many quarters, defines itself as countercultural. Its experience of so many ideologies and divisions has made it wry and circumspect. Perhaps so much history has had just a little influence on the capital's sense of humour, the much-renowned *Berliner Schnauze*, or Berlin sass (*Schnauze* means 'muzzle', like a dog's). Berliners can be very friendly, but at times you get an insult masquerading as humour, such as when a waiter tests you (*Trinkgeld sonst Schnauze,* 'tip or you get sass'), or a shopkeeper quips that you should shut the door behind you (*Biste in de S-Bahn jebor'n oder wat?* 'Were you born in the S-Bahn or what?'). Berliners will assure you that behind the insult there is *Herz* ('heart'). But perhaps you notice there is something else behind the character of their wit – a toughness, an admirable resilience. I can't help but think of those endless forests, depths of sand and dark winter days, and the mounds of rubble that needed to be cleared away to create something new.

In the summer, with its long nights, Berlin transforms, and youth culture goes outside. This park is in Kreuzberg.

THE CITY TODAY

The Spacious City

Berlin is Europe's greenest capital. More than eight times the size of Paris proper with only one and a half times its population, Berlin fills its relative excess with trees, such as street-side lindens and maples. The city, depopulated by war and division, feels spacious, with the horizon often visible. The largeness can frighten some visitors, who find themselves alone on a street corner of a boulevard at night, in the centre of the city, confronted by depopulated gloom. They might wonder whether this could possibly be Germany's most dynamic hub, or instead one of those provincial places to which administrators are relegated: a Brasilia, an Ottawa or – gasp – a Bonn. For the metropolitan, you can smell the countryside a little too often in Berlin. For others, this release from the usual city noise and claustrophobia is a liberation, because in Berlin you have the advantage of a capital's attitude and infrastructure without the inconvenience of metropolitan stress. Frank O'Hara would have found Berlin as reassuring as New York, when writing: 'I can't even enjoy a blade of grass unless I know there's a subway handy.'

The massive transport network, built for a metropolis that was much larger in the 1930s than today in terms of population, reinforces the experience of the city's emptiness, with all those vacant train cars and platforms. As you depart the touristic heart of Mitte and Kreuzberg, you may wonder what happened to all the people. Perhaps you will have a sobering moment, and reflect on how many people fled or died here. The superstitious might imagine all those empty seats occupied by ghosts.

Berlin is the European city most like its New World counterparts: its domesticated leafy suburbs most resemble those in Chicago or Toronto; its rambling vastness can be compared to a Los Angeles but with effective public transport; the heterogeneity of its urban style resembles New York. It is not a tightly spun knot of monuments and historic boulevards, like Paris or Prague. It is instead a city blown open by bombs and post-1945 planning, of highways and high-rise housing projects. It is this eclecticism and low density that leads people to say Berlin is not a beautiful city, but an interesting one. Its population is spread thinly across these spaces, far exceeding the city limits: the greater metropolitan area has approximately six million.

Within this sprawl, there is as yet no single centre. Historic Cölln-Berlin is located entirely in the former East near Alexanderplatz ('Alex'), while West Berlin has its centre around Zoologischer Garten ('Zoo'). Even before the city's post-war division, East and West were shorthand for different poles of the city.

Alexanderplatz today.

The area around Alex had much of the urban poverty; trade winds carried the bad air of coal and smoke east, towards the square and the factories huddled down the Spree river. Near Zoo were the upmarket shops of Tauentzienstrasse and Kurfürstendamm.

When the Wall was built, poor and rich found themselves largely in the historically proletarian and bourgeois centres of East and West Berlin respectively. And then when the Wall fell, peripheral West Berlin neighbourhoods, Kreuzberg and Neukölln, suddenly found themselves adjacent to the city's Eastern heart. Kreuzberg is erroneously presumed by many tourists to have once been part of East Berlin! The two centres – Alex and Zoo – then struggled like huge stars to capture the neighbourhoods between them in their gravitational force, to achieve dominance as the nucleus of a united capital. Even boroughs adjacent to the old centre of the West, like

Alexanderplatz at the turn of the 20th century.

Schöneberg, found themselves turning towards Alex – a phenomenon that can be best seen in the spread of rental prices from the East's now expensive core, decreasing through its dependent planets, before rising again as one reaches the old-money West. The G-force of Mitte, or the Old East, has been responsible, of course, for many of Berlin's most pressing problems of gentrification and rising rental prices.

And yet even to talk of two hubs is misleading, because if one were to visit either, one would be disappointed by the lack of city life, their deadness at night, the fact that nothing really goes on in Alex other than cinemas and shopping, and nothing really goes on at Zoo apart from . . . cinemas and shopping. In this respect, Berlin is again not so different from many of its American counterparts, except that this desolation is not accompanied by extreme social problems of violence and poverty. It is also possible to claim that there are other centres in the city, including one at the boundary between former West and East, the new corporate high-rise 'downtown' around Potsdamer Platz. It's a place that imparts the charm of a suburban research park combined with a sprawling mall, constructed vertically, not so different from La Défense in Paris, but in the city's geographic heart.

Most of the city's life happens in the neighbourhoods, in a way that is comparable to London. If the city is like the night sky, where it's easy to get lost in the dark places between, it is also dotted with many stars, places of life, called, using the terminology of Berlinerisch, the *Kiez*. The *Kieze*, or 'hoods', should be immediately distinguished from the *Bezirke*, which are larger administrative entities or boroughs. Talking about Covent Garden is different from talking about the City of Westminster, just as the *Kieze* of Cobble Hill or Park Slope differ from the *Bezirk* of Brooklyn. Each *Kiez* is named after a high street that runs through it, often full of commerce, restaurants and bars. You can perceptibly feel yourself entering a *Kiez* when walking through Berlin: from the lonely abandonment of empty streets, you turn a corner and enter an avenue with many more people. Property prices too reflect proximity to the centre of these various *Kieze*, and one of the fabled pieces of

Berlin property advice, akin to 'location location location', is 'live in a *Kiez*'. Talking about Berlin in terms of 'Kreuzberg' is then rather vague in comparison to talking about living in the 'Graefe-*kiez*' (that vibrant area of Kreuzberg near U-Bahn Schönleinstrasse). 'Kreuzberg' might as well refer to one of the streets by the Jewish Museum, where a walk outside at night involves a disheartening journey between 1960s block housing and empty scrubby lots. Meanwhile, each *Kiez* has its peculiar character, and two located within a short walking distance of one another, even within the same *Bezirk*, can have completely different attitudes.

For this reason, it is very easy to get Berlin 'wrong' on a short visit. I remember meeting one visiting Canadian couple who had spent a week in the city and managed to spend their time avoiding all the *Kieze* and only hitting the 'empty' parts. 'We're great walkers, we walk everywhere,' they told me, but obviously they had walked between all the stars of Berlin's night sky. This experience left them disconsolate that dark and rainy November, without any plans for a return visit. Berlin is a city where you cannot simply launch out. You need to know where you are going. The same goes for Berliners: it is the city of listing magazines (*Zitty, tip Berlin*, *Siegessäule*), blogs (Cee Cee, überlin and mine, The Needle) and word of mouth. How else does one know that down that empty street, located well outside a *Kiez*, there might be – through the fourth portal to the left, in the basement of the second courtyard, at the end of the hallway turn right – five hundred people dancing to the world's finest electronic music? Berlin can seem soulless, empty, dead, frightening, if you don't know on which door to knock.

The combination of these various peculiarities of the city's shape makes Berlin unique in relation to other European metropolises. The breezy greenness, parks and the fact that you can see the sky conquer claustrophobia. The sprawl and depopulation give an element of surprise, a constant feeling of discovery in the vast patchwork. No place in the city dominates; centres compete but are in fact empty, while neighbourhoods gain more importance. Perhaps all this tells one something, after all, about Germany: Berlin is not the country's industrial or financial hub, just one of many competing conurbations (among Munich, Frankfurt, Cologne and Hamburg), but one increasingly making its centrality felt. The enduring lack of centre gives one a liberating feeling: that there is no standard; there is no radius by which to measure distance. There is no place, neither in Germany nor its capital, where you can stand – as in the courtyard of the Louvre, which feels like the centre of a whole country and that country's centralized idea of itself and its manners – and say this is Germany, or this is Berlin.

Understanding the whole in relation to its parts is a classic philosophical problem. This is why today we should walk the city to see its *Bezirke* and *Kieze*. And since there is no one single obvious place to start, why not begin with the green expanses to the west of the city, where the Havel and Spree rivers widen to a region of lakes and parks still within the city limits, and two of the most popular of such lakes, Wannsee and Schlachtensee.

Memory and Nature

Wannsee and Schlachtensee are two lakes close to each other in the former West Berlin, one large and one small. They are connected to the river systems of the Spree and Havel, as are the lakes Grunewaldsee, Krumme Lanke and Nikolassee. Fringed by leaning trees, their gently curving shores are close to the border between Berlin and Brandenburg. Not far are the Prussian palaces of Potsdam, and Friedrich Wilhelm II's pleasure island, the Peacock Island or *Pfaueninsel*, with its follies, exotic birds and a Marie Antoinette-esque buttery. I like to come to these lakes in the early morning, when the men from the *Biergarten* are washing down the tables, waiting for the arrival of swimmers, boaters and families of Berlin's West. But now there is no one about. There are just the trees trailing their branches in the waterways.

Wannsee is known for its villas on the lake. One belonged to the artist Max Liebermann and his widow before the Nazis forced her to sell the house in 1940. She would commit suicide rather than let the Gestapo take her away. Only a few hundred metres along the lakeshore is the House of the Wannsee Conference where, on 20 January 1942, an important meeting took place to implement the euphemistic 'Final Solution' of the Jewish Question across Europe.

One can visit the Wannsee Conference Villa today. It is a museum of the Holocaust. What is most attractive about the ghastly villa, with its stuccoed classicism and overgrown *putti*, is its gardens and the elegant view of boaters and swimmers. Walk down the lawn to the lake's edge, and there is a band of red flowers, and lily pads floating in the water. Across from them, on the other side of the lake, is a massive bathing installation, Strandbad Wannsee, built mostly in the 1920s, but then Aryanized by the Nazis who wished to organize the leisure time of its *Volk*.

The corporality of the Wannsee lakeside is best seen in the photographs of Will McBride (1931–2015), who came to Germany with the U.S. Army. Arriving in Berlin in 1955, at the age of 24, he observed the city's reconstruction on the front line of the Cold War. It is precisely the human body at leisure, going about weekend activities, in a city scarred by the traces of recent cataclysmic political events, that is so compelling in his work. A 1958 photograph from Wannsee shows young bathers competing in a betting game, *The Bottle Game at Strandbad Wannsee*. Another, from 1959, *Eating Popcorn at Strandbad Wannsee*, shows a young man with an emaciated chest holding a kernel to his lips, while one woman is poised to smoke her cigarette, and another has her mouth full.

I cannot help but think simultaneously about all those fragile bathers and the murderous plan to destroy human bodies, decreed by pen-stroke, which was endorsed in the villa behind. I cannot help but conflate these things, and feel that nature is contaminated too. Those flowers at the lake

Schlachtensee, a lake in the west of Berlin.

Will McBride, *Eating Popcorn at Strandbad Wannsee*, Berlin, 1959.

edge have a blush of blood, those tendrils of water lilies are somehow monstrous.

But I stop myself, because how can the trees be guilty, how can the water in Wannsee be implicated in a meeting of high-ranking bureaucrats some 75 years ago? For me, Wannsee is shorthand for murder, but come here on a sunny summer day and one can only remark on the humanism of so much open space for recreation and enjoyment. And, yet, something about the idea of nature being wholly indifferent to such history fills me too with unease, as if I am entirely unsynchronized with my surroundings. The quiet physical beauty of this corner of Berlin is in tension with the memory of the Holocaust, whose fleeting horror does not exist in nature – one must strive to keep it alive in the mind.

I take the S-Bahn three stops to nearby Mexikoplatz, passing many great villas. My partner jokes that the station near Schlachtensee, with its art nouveau dome dating from 1904, and the surrounding streets (such as Argentinische Allee), are named after South American places so that 'when grandfather returns from hiding in Latin America he'll feel quite at home.' In fact, many of the most important members of the Nazi hierarchy lived in the borough Steglitz-Zehlendorf, including Albert Speer, who resided just south of the lake, and Goebbels, who bought a cut-price villa at Schwanenwerder at the top of the Wannsee. Walking down Limastrasse towards Schlachtensee, I see an enormous faux-Alpine construction, and wonder who might have called in for dinner. But, of course, this neighbourhood was also traditionally popular with Jews; victims often lived next door to perpetrators. In Christopher Isherwood's *Goodbye to Berlin*, it is to a Wannsee villa that his mysterious friend Bernard Landauer takes him, it seems, for a tryst.

Today the neighbourhood is quiet, wealthy, bourgeois, comfortable. Some Americans live here to be close to the JFK School. Academics find it is not so far from Dahlem and the Free University. It is suburban, quiet in winter and busy in summer, when the S-Bahn line fills with families and bicycles, and empties them on the lake shores. More arrive by the cycle paths, through the vast forests dappled with sunlight, from the centre of the city.

Schlachtensee is well-heeled and quite international, compared to the much larger bathing experience of Wannsee, or the lakes still separately visited by East Berliners across the former boundary. Weekenders stretch out on the slopes of the lake, going down to shore, lazing under the canopies of branches, sometimes naked, with their picnic lunches, their bottles of wine, cured meats and cheeses. They bathe in the clear waters that grow muddier as the summer wears on. Dogs used to run loose and shake droplets over the picnic blankets until the city imposed a ban (encouraging wild boars to come out of hiding). A fit group of runners makes another circle. There are fleets of Berlin high school kids who flirt between canoes, while an old woman swims the 200-metre width of the lake, and back, repeatedly.

She seems unperturbed by Schlachtensee's monster. Ever since medieval times, there has been evidence of the giant *Wels*, an enormous lake catfish 2 metres long that infrequently bites swimmers (in 2008 a woman suffered a 20-centimetre-long wound, or so reported a local hospital). Local lore has it that it does not simply leave bite marks on its victims, but can swallow children whole. I am reminded of a

Bathers at Schlachtensee.

scene from Hans Fallada's *Alone in Berlin* when a Gestapo inspector watches his victim, who has been shot, fall into this lake: 'the heavy body smacked into the water and straightaway disappeared. Better that way! [the *Gestapo* agent] said to himself, as he moistened his dry lips. Less evidence.' Did he hope that the carp would feast on the remains?

At the beer garden of the old Fischerhütte – a structure that has reportedly been there in many forms since the seventeenth century – the Sunday lake-goers balance half-litre glasses of lager, with sausages, *Bretzel* and potato salad, on plastic trays. I walk inside the building; the restaurant is as fancy as the service is deplorable and disorganized, and there are a number of historical photos, which were until recently displayed at the top of the stairwell.

There is one from the war years, of the Fischerhütte in 1940. The tables are set with fine china and crystal, but the places are not yet occupied. To see the dining room deserted in that year leaves me with an eerie feeling. I feel anticipation for the guests to arrive, but we will not see them. The sense of expectancy seems shared; the guests I think must be speculating about what lies ahead with the new war. I now know what these guests would like to know. They might all be ghosts by now.

But what strikes me most about the photograph is the view to the lake, through the dining room windows. It has remained unchanged. Just looking at it, we could be in the twenty-first century, or 1940.

I had only considered nature's indifference to human events. But, here, nature unexpectedly provides continuity. Looking from the image to the landscape, and back, it's as if I have walked into the past. The view connects the past to the present, and the missing guests to us. And yet the lake remains entirely indifferent as to when the photograph was taken. I am still waiting for the waters to speak.

The Resurrection of the Dead

Soon after I moved to Berlin, I wrote in my blog about the Old West as 'expensive, boring, bourgeois quarters full of elderly people', and faced a barrage of criticism from denizens of these neighbourhoods, commenting that I had overlooked their cultural contributions and diversity. I countered with statistics: the average age here is 46, compared to Kreuzberg and Friedrichshain where it is a full decade younger. I joked, 'Have you been to Wilmersdorf? Have you seen the film *Children of Men*?' It wasn't long, however, before the *Götter* decided that I would have to spend part of my working life on the border between Charlottenburg and Wilmersdorf, and I would get to know the *Bezirke* rather better than I had initially expected. Predictably, my opinion about the neighbourhood changed as well.

One reason the Old West has always been important, and will remain important, is location. Berliners often talk about the city within the *Ring* or *Ringbahn*, the S-Bahn line that circles the city for 37 km. It now carries a half-million passengers daily, but it already existed as an interrupted rail circuit by 1877. Torn apart by the Wall in 1961, the West had only just started dismantling the *Ringbahn* in the 1980s, only to have to rebuild it again, opening it in 2002 as a complete circle. It's a sign of just how unexpected reunification was. If there's a wall in today's city, it is the *Ringbahn*: it is more permeable than Paris's *périphérique*, but tighter and more psychologically present than London's M25. The Old West is that neighbourhood that stretches from inside the western *Ring* right to the Tiergarten in the city's geographical heart, making it some of the most desirable property in the new Berlin.

The boulevard of Kurfürstendamm intersects with the *Ring* at S-Bahn Halensee. From here, one can make the long 3-kilometre march through the centre of the Old West to the Kaiser Wilhelm Memorial Church. The Kurfürstendamm is too grand and too long to belong to, and so name, a single *Kiez*. It gets progressively ostentatious as you follow its wide pavement, leaving behind the Old West island provincialism – Italian restaurants with red-checked tablecloths and cake shops with lace in the windows – for French bistros and cafés attached to hotels like the Kempinski,

The Kurfürstendamm in winter.

surrounded by brand-name luxury stores such as Prada, Gucci and Fendi.

I follow the Kurfürstendamm to the Schaubühne, which is arguably Germany's most internationally recognized theatre, where I have been writing essays about productions for a few years. It's only a few hundred metres east from Halensee. The building was the old 'Universum' cinema designed by the architect Erich Mendelsohn in 1928, as part of a multi-use project that included shops, apartments, a restaurant and a

Lars Eidinger as Richard III in Thomas Ostermeier's production at the Schaubühne.

cabaret. It has a graceful flying-saucer curve of a facade, the kind that might have inspired Oscar Niemeyer. Partly destroyed in the war, the space was remodelled for the Schaubühne in 1981.

Walk through the doorway and sit in the windowed café, where groups of thespians knock back their lunches of Snickers, *Wiener Würstchen* (hot dogs) loaded with mustard, and a bag of crisps – known at the canteen as the 'dramaturge's special'. Much of the theatre's life happens in this café space: a director sitting in the corner talking to a journalist with her Dictaphone between them on the table; actors mouthing words to themselves as they imbibe more coffee; and then those same personalities after shows ordering – why not? – yet another *Weissweinschorle* as they question how much better or worse the dress rehearsal was compared to the premiere. One might expect to see the grey-haired set dominate here, but in fact one quickly realizes the obvious: that the many young people here were born in the leafy suburbs of West Berlin to those same old people. Well-groomed products of *Bildung*, or general education, you can see them descend to the theatre in the evening, joined by people from all over the country.

The doors might be closed, but you can look through the glass down the long hallway leading to the performance spaces. One is a 'Globe Theatre' based on Shakespeare's in London, with a stage that juts into the audience, inaugurated by artistic director Thomas Ostermeier's *Richard III* in 2015, starring the devilish film and theatre star and sometime DJ Lars Eidinger. Internationally, the Schaubühne is perhaps known for putting naked bodies on stage (Eidinger reading Puck's final speech with his penis, or taking a sausage up his bottom), although Ostermeier and playwright/director Marius von Mayenburg are kicking against the expectation that they represent the 'blood and sperm' generation, and engaging in a broader range of production: delicate *Kammerspiele* or dark comedies. The directors might retire after performances upstairs to a labyrinth of white winding corridors, with a floor plan made wonky by bombing. The austerity resembles Tarkovsky in outer space, from which one might never return across the 'fourth wall'. Meanwhile, all the other big state-funded theatres are in the former East – the embattled Volksbühne (the current target of an overhaul by Berlin's culture tsars), the Deutsches Theater, Brecht's old Berliner Ensemble and the Gorky Theater.

From Adenauerplatz, if one were to take a sharp left, one would get an explanation for all the Russian one hears in this part of town. This community has given the quarter the nick-name 'Charlottengrad'. At the Charlottenburg S-Bahn station (on the east–west line) there is a 24-hour Russian supermarket, Rossia, which sells everything from Cheburashka dolls to an extensive selection of vodka, buckwheat, frozen *vareniki* and beers with remarkable alcohol percentages. Outside, men grill *shashlik* meat skewers for the canteen and pile the plates with flat bread and onions. It's as if the entire place is a waiting room for the Moscow–Paris night train that rolls overhead, except that the train doesn't stop, and the Russians here do not necessarily want to get on. And it's not just because it takes 21 hours to get to Smolensk (direct!).

Russians have been coming to this part of Berlin since the Revolution, as a place of exile and refuge. The man at the cash register of Rossia tells me he is a Russian-speaking German from Kazakhstan, and that he arrived with the population of *Wolgadeutsch* at the time of reunification. Russians who can trace their German roots back to the time of Catherine the Great were granted German citizenship, on no criteria except for blood, and many came to Berlin. Conspicuously, they chose the former Western half, eschewing all Eastern connections. Many presume Russians in Berlin are today's oligarchs spending money in the high-end shops, living it big in a Western capital not far from Moscow. But those perspiring women in fur coats with small dogs browsing in the Louis Vuitton store account for only a small part of Berlin's 100,000-strong Russian community. The most recent émigré community is Russia's gay population. The Berlin NGO Quarteera is active in providing advice to gay people threatened by homophobic legislation in Russia, who can seek asylum in Germany based on their sexual orientation.

Wilmersdorf and Charlottenburg, at this point, do not live up to the stereotypes of being particularly aged, culturally sterile or lacking in diversity. And Charlottenburg does not stoop to comparisons with other *Bezirke*, having been established in its own right in 1705, and even considered a *Grossstadt* of more than 100,000 since the 1890s. Only with the 1920 Berlin Act was it absorbed into the City of Berlin. The heart of Charlottenburg is the eighteenth-century Charlottenburg Palace, and across from it the old *Garde du Corps* villa, which now houses a very beautiful collection of Klees, Picassos and Matisses, donated to the city in 1996 by one of the Old West's most famous Jewish families, the Berggruens.

The family history is international and complex. Born in Wilmersdorf in 1914, Heinz Berggruen escaped the Nazis in 1936, studied in Berkeley, and was active in the art scene of San Francisco, where he had an affair with Frida Kahlo while curating her husband Diego Rivera's drawings. He only returned to Germany with the U.S. Army during the Second World War. In 1947 he opened a bookshop on the Île St-Louis and became friends with Picasso, collecting 131 of his works. Late in life, he said, 'Understanding and tolerance are traditional Jewish virtues . . . One can no longer turn one's back

A restaurant popular with the Russian community in 'Charlottengrad'.

on the country of Dürer and Goethe, Beethoven and Brahms, Gottfried Benn and Max Beckmann.' His gift of 'reconciliation' to his birthplace was his private collection, which he sold to Berlin for a fraction of its value. He lived at the top of the circular staircase of the old villa, coming down at times to admire his artwork among the ticket holders, and passed away in 2007. His son, Nicolas, is now the world's most famous 'homeless billionaire', living out of hotel rooms without a fixed address.

Back on the Kurfürstendamm, one walks past the high-end shops, the colonnaded *fin de siècle* facade of Cumberland House with its gaudy café, Old World hotels with a touch of the 1950s, knife shops, the BMW emporium, the gold merchants, and at the corner of Fasanenstrasse one can look to the crusty *Literaturhaus* in its garden. All around is the flurry of post-war mercantilism, because we are in the old British Western zone, the first to redevelop after the war when the rubble was cleared. It became a window of capitalist consumption, and it was the first place on which many *Ossis* descended after the Wall fell, to browse previously untouchable, and for the most part still unaffordable, Western products at the nearby KaDeWe

A vintage West Berlin taxi.

department store on Tauentzienstrasse, the old *flâneur* stretch of Kästner and Isherwood.

I sometimes feel distinctly odd shopping in a neighbourhood where there are so many reminders of Germany's dark past. I understand the admittedly insensitive quip of an acquaintance that he hates going to the Old West because it is all 'chain stores and memorials to the dead'. The most conspicuous site of remembrance, at the corner of Tauentzienstrasse and Kurfürstendamm, is the 1895 Kaiser Wilhelm Memorial Church, once dubbed the *Taufhaus des Westens* (the 'baptistry of the West') to match KaDeWe's *Kaufhaus des Westens* (or 'confiserie of the West'). It is perhaps the ugliest church in Berlin, improved, as one historian noted, only by bombing in 1943. It now purposefully remains in a ruined state (ruins that paradoxically needed recent restoration) as a warning of the horror of war, and was the site of the December 2016 Christmas Market attack which killed one dozen people and wounded scores. Just in front of KaDeWe, at Wittenbergplatz, there is a more discreet memorial at the station: a series of destinations posted for passengers. They are not the expected stations on the U1 line, but rather Auschwitz, Treblinka and other Nazi camps. A similar project exists in Grunewald, on the train platform (Gleis 17) where victims embarked to their deaths. Yes, many of these memorials find themselves in the cadre of what feels now like an almost vintage consumerism, but nonetheless it was here, in the former West, where most of the self-critical 'coming to terms with the past', or *Vergangenheitsbewältigung*, happened, a laudable process of national reckoning with few international parallels.

Many are now talking about 'the rediscovery of the Old West'. It is time for the area around Zoologischer Garten to catch up, for it to replace those seedy but charming sex shops with high-end multi-billion projects, such as the new Waldorf Astoria. The recent Bikini Mall, with its view of the Zoo's monkey enclosure, appeals to a younger fashion-conscious generation, offering Mykita eyeglasses and modernist furniture knock-offs, with some lonely-looking pop-ups to keep it 'real'. It repackages the Berlin 'cool' born in the East, but in a domesticated mall space more familiar to West Berlin shoppers. Bikini is nonetheless a loving renovation of a 1955–7 modernist building, and elsewhere in West Berlin there is a rediscovery of high modernism – the refit of the Zoo Palast Cinema of 1957 and the arrival of the C/O photography gallery in Amerika House of the same year. If West Berlin still feels like an aged relic of the pre-*Wende* times, this will not last long given aggressive property development of everything inside the *Ringbahn*. The emergent style tells us something too about the direction of Berlin. Much of what is new in the Old West is carefully packaged for gallerists and entrepreneurs who are nostalgic about living in an elegant, consumer-oriented, well-tailored European capital – a commercial rebuttal to the shabby, anti-consumerist and alternative 'cool' that for so many years was found farther east.

The Tiergarten at the turn of the 20th century.

War Damage

How best to reconstruct a city that was largely destroyed? When the Wall came down, Berlin's historic centre was revealed behind it, still not fully repaired from the damage of the Second World War. The East Germans had 'improved' the centre with Socialist constructions, but there were facades still scarred with shrapnel, buildings full of rubble and an inordinate number of empty lots. A stroll today from the Tiergarten down Unter den Linden to Alexanderplatz is arguably the most compelling of any European capital, precisely because there are so many layers of historical reconstruction. One can clearly see the different techniques used to repair the city from the damage of its competing rulers, ideologies and defeats, competing visions of how cities should be brought back from the dead.

When I wander through the Tiergarten – or 'Garden of Beasts', the hunting grounds of the Prussian kings – I am struck by how it, like so many natural spaces in the city, creates the impression of timelessness. And yet a careful botanical eye notices that few trees are more than 65 years old. The park was devastated by the war, and almost entirely denuded of firewood in the cold winter of 1946; the equestrian statues were left randomly studding the horizon, deprived of their central places among the gardens. The Zoo animals had already been butchered by starving Berliners for their meat: you could buy zebra and lion on the black market during the war. The park – this once wild space in the city, as much a subject of lore and fascination, emotional connection and pride as Central Park is to New York – was then domesticated as a giant vegetable garden for the hungry Berliners of the post-war period until the trees were regrown in the 1950s. The Tiergarten has since matured: but, like many buildings destroyed by war, it is a reconstruction.

I sometimes wonder how a park regrows after war differently from a building. What if we could plant a single stone of a ruined palace, wait a few decades, and see it sprout again into its former shape? A park regenerates itself, but the age of the trees tell us how much time has passed. How are buildings, destroyed by war, restored so that they too show time passing?

The forest surrounds the centres of power of a newly confident German democracy. Numerous embassies front the Tiergarten, with diplomats retreating into the park for private conversation, giving it an air of conspiracy and intrigue. And at the opposite side of the green, the Reichstag (1894) looms behind the branches. The original architect Paul Wallot wanted to project not only legitimacy and power, with stolid classical pillars, but the Reich's industrial might, using new technologies for a glass and steel dome. Remarkably, the shell of the building, the site of room-to-room combat in the final hours of the Second World War, survived the conflict, but its dome was close to collapse. It was this architectural element that would be the centre point of reconstruction after reunification, a long process involving the wrapping of the building in luminous polypropylene fabric by the artist Christo in 1995 – a kind of symbolic transformation, a Lazarus moment for the heavy and pompous building that had figured so prominently in German history. The new dome, part of the conversion led by British architect Norman Foster, is a double helix of ramps rising around a mirrored cone, where visitors spiral up for a view over Berlin. They symbolically stand over a transparent panel looking down at the German chamber. The interior of the building below, meanwhile, was not reconstructed as it was before 1933; damaged elements were replaced with glass and steel. Visitors to the chamber can sit close enough to members of parliament to read their notes. While one might debate the symbolism – whether government's relationship to citizens is really so transparent – the building nonetheless expresses an

The Victoria Café, at Unter den Linden 46. In the early 20th century, the avenue was bustling and inhabited. After the bombing and the division, museums, embassies and car showrooms took over.

ethos of openness and democracy, the transformation of the character of German government necessary to placate international suspicions at the time of reunification.

From the Brandenburg Gate, Unter den Linden presents a series of historic facades, behind which lurk souvenir shops, embassies, automobile showrooms and kitsch historical cafés. A few streets behind the avenue is the elegant square Gendarmenmarkt. Further down the boulevard is the majestic Forum Fridericianum. There, on Bebelplatz, is a subterranean monument to the 1933 book burning, which is simply a poignant set of empty bookshelves.

At the far end of Unter den Linden, one reaches one of the world's more remarkable complexes of museums, positioned on the island that was Berlin's original settlement. Old Cölln is hard to fathom today, so thoroughly levelled was it, first by imperial plans to make the island a showcase, and then by war bombing and the subsequent city planning of the Communists. The Museum Island is not merely a set of remarkable art and archaeology collections housed in stunning Neoclassical buildings. It says something too about Berlin's preoccupation with the past. In fact, two competing theories of how to restore Berlin battle on opposite sides of the island.

The Museum Island was initiated by Karl Friedrich Schinkel's Altes Museum (1823–30), a long colonnaded building that faces across the square to the Berliner Cathedral or *Dom* (a godless city deserves such a godless building) and the Berliner Schloss (City Palace, or city residence of the Hohenzollerns). Together they form a trinity of Culture, Religion and Kingdom. The Altes Museum looks again to classical forms for legitimacy, and inside contains ancient Greek and Roman sculpture collections. It was the architect Friedrich August Stüler who expanded on the 'Old' Museum by creating his 'New' or Neues Museum in 1849. The remarkable Pergamon Museum, meanwhile, is one of the world's most important archaeological complexes, with its Hellenistic altar and ancient gates of Babylon. The Alte

Shattered frescoes depicting the sites of German archaeological digs in the Near East, in the Neues Museum.

Nationalgalerie contains nineteenth-century masterworks, such as a room of unsettling and melancholic Caspar David Friedrich landscapes. And the Bode Museum has sculpture, and a remarkable mosaic chapel from Ravenna, which stares down through the tall windows in winter to ice cracking in the Spree. Five museums in all now complete the Museum Island. The city is connecting them through a single entrance now being built along the Spree, which will create a unified UNESCO-listed complex to rival the Louvre in Paris.

The Neues Museum is the most compelling structure on the island: it houses the Egyptian collection, as well as the palaeontological and early 'German' collections. The comparison between Northern and Southern antiquity cannot help but show up the primitiveness of German prehistory, where a rude hammered conical golden hat from the Bronze Age (1000 BC) cannot rival the mysterious and arch elegance of the world-famous mask of Nefertiti (from 1345 BC).

The restoration of the Neues Museum was completed by the British architect David Chipperfield (1953–), who remarked on how much Germans 'like to discuss' during the lengthy eleven-year project. The idea was to 'conserve' but not to 'restore'. Chipperfield compared the process to piecing back together a shattered amphora, although some of the pieces had been lost. Indeed, the Neues Museum suffered more than any other building on the island, especially in November 1943 and February 1945. After the War, it was a thrilling place into which to sneak and explore the remains. From September 1989 conservation began in earnest on 'Europe's biggest ever Humpty Dumpty project' – one that would show and preserve evidence of war damage. This is the most dramatic aspect for today's visitor: the contrast between white new spaces and the charred and shattered remains that are riddled with bullet and shrapnel holes. There is a recognition here that the museum does not abridge a painful past, but rather includes it as a process. I find nothing so poignant here as seeing objects from the distant past in a space that itself reflects on the passage of time. The German ideal of exploration and colonialism also lies here in ruins: the romantic nineteenth-century friezes of German archaeological digs in the Near East are shattered before the cracked remains of mummies' tombs. It is a palace of broken dreams and empires ending.

While both the Reichstag and the Neues Museum allow war damage to remain visible, the approach to the past could not be more different across the Lustgarten, where a Baroque palace is being rebuilt from the ground up. At the time of writing (autumn 2016), a huge concrete shell had arisen, partially covered with a sculpted facade, topped by a Baroque dome. The internal structure looks comical because it is made with the same material one might use for, say, a multi-storey car park. A hybrid facade is already being built over this effigy: the front is a copy of the Berliner Schloss (City Palace, Palace of the Hohenzollern), while the back is more contemporary, partly as a cost-cutting measure (it looks more inspired by Albert Speer than anything else on the island).

There are two major points of contention for this €600 million project, financed with mostly federal funds. The first regards the history of the site: the original Baroque palace, damaged by war, met its end in 1950 when the East Germans

The foundations of the Berlin City Palace before rebuilding, 2010.

detonated it, removing the old symbol of Prussian and imperial militarism and power from the new Socialist State. Between 1976 and 1994, the lot was the site of the Palast der Republik (Palace of the Republic), the East German seat of government. It met its end with reunification and was destroyed completely by 2008, seemingly because of an asbestos risk. For many East Germans, however, who had fond memories of the social spaces in the building, the reunified Germany's rationale for the destruction of the Palast der Republik was not so different from the East Germans' detonation of the Schloss: the elimination of the symbols of a former power, the deletion of a past state by a present state. The accusation that there has been an official policy of forgetting, a conquest of the West over East, is a major source of contention.

The second problem is that of 'abridgement': the present project is not the building of something new, as the Palast der Republik was in its period, but rather a return to the pre-Second World War period as if the intervening years had not occurred, as if the Baroque palace had not met its fate under the East Germans in 1950. This raises questions about whether Berlin is symbolically returning to the militarism of the Prussian and imperial period, and the Nazi period that followed it, in rebuilding the palace. The impressive anthropological collections from the Dahlem museums will be transferred to the gallery spaces of the palace, and many ask whether colonial loot should be placed in a symbol of German imperial power. Is such a gesture appropriate in the twenty-first century? This abridgement – to a time of expansion and imperialism, one that makes a parenthesis of much of the twentieth century and rehabilitates the imperial heritage – is something of a reversal of the treatment of memory in the Neues Museum. The difference in the plans for these two museums on the island epitomizes the struggle over memory in the German capital today.

The historical moment that the City Palace abridges is that of the Communists, who themselves (like their modernist counterparts in the West) had a destructive impulse towards the past in the immediate post-war period. The East German national anthem, 'Auferstanden aus Ruinen' ('Rising from the Ruins'), extolled German youth and a paradisiacal future. The State did embark later, however, on a number of quite perverse reconstruction projects, such as that of the Nikolaiviertel, the old historic area of Cölln, remade between 1980 and 1987 largely with *Plattenbau* architecture in the medieval style (*Platten* are panels prefabricated in factories, brought in flat on trucks and assembled like Lego pieces, with obvious seams, and were used to construct mass housing all over the GDR). But the original impulse was to detonate the past, to make way for yet another form of imperium while creating open spaces and much-needed housing.

The area around Alexanderplatz was almost completely reconfigured, in a manner that reminds one today of *The Jetsons*, or other vintage examples of how the future was imagined by people in the past. The Centrum Warenhaus (now the Galleria Kaufhaus) rose with a crinkly white mesh facade, looking down at fountains resembling radioactive mushrooms. Not far away was the World Clock (1969), with its rickety rotating model of the planets, under which East Germans could read the time in all the places they were not allowed to visit. Behind the square begins the Stalinist Karl-Marx-Allee, a boulevard meant for tanks, so broad an aircraft could land on it. Its stern socialist-Classical architecture is dotted with marvellous modernist concrete and glass pavilions, and the swooping 1963 facade of the Kino International cinema. But if one structure were to represent the entire socialist complex it must be the watchful eye of Alexanderplatz's Fernsehturm, 'Television Tower', of 1969, the second highest structure in Europe at 368 metres, with its futuristic bed of jutting wings, popular with skateboarders. Today the needle's uplit sphere resembles a giant disco ball overseeing the capital's shenanigans, and no longer representing the grim surveillance of a paranoid state. But still today, one cannot help but feel that the socialist future was technological and otherworldly, dwarfing its citizens.

From the dramatic viewing platform of the Fernsehturm, on a clear day, one has a stunning view back towards the

Tiergarten. The entire monumental avenue of Unter den Linden stretches from the Museum Island to the Brandenburg Gate like a model. One realizes rapidly, at this height, how many empty spaces are still left over in the city's heart – not just from the war, but from division and deindustrialization – how many cranes have been raised, and how many more choices still need to be made. At the base of the tower, there are plans for redevelopment around the massive scrappy square between the isolated steeple of the medieval Marienkirche and the Red City Hall. Before the war, this was a densely populated city centre neighbourhood, and developers are keen to make this prime property profitable. The construction works of the U5 extension stretch along Unter den Linden, part of a project to connect the city's heart to the wider underground system. One sees, looking south along the river, deindustrialized land that property investors are eager to convert into the 'Mediaspree' and 'Mercedes-Benz Quarter', a high-rise corporate media district. Which one of the existing and competing examples of how the past has been either incorporated, abridged or destroyed will prevail here?

At times I am nostalgic – perhaps like those private contributors to the Berliner Schloss project – and like to think that the dense old heart of the medieval town could just reappear, budding over the soulless highway of Leipziger Strasse, or along the once-picturesque canals. But you can't just plant a stone.

The Berlin Diaspora

How can you live in Berlin if you know about its history?' a student once asked me. 'How can you walk down the streets knowing what horrors happened here?' We were strolling into the area near Hackescher Markt from the Museum Island into some of the oldest remaining streets of the city: narrow ways fronted by eighteenth-century residential houses, courtyards hidden behind courtyards, with artisanal workshops, cafés, intimate bars and galleries. The streets are also full of people taking photographs, with guidebooks under their arms. This part of Mitte – in and around the Barn District, since for fire protection the barns were located just outside the first city walls – became the centre of Jewish life in Berlin until the Second World War.

Between Alexanderplatz and Hackescher Markt, which is now the location for a great deal of high-end retail and hotel development, there is a little street called Rosenstrasse. The square, like so many in Berlin, is not very promising: there is a Spanish-language centre, tall-growing grasses, scrappy trees, a mix of post-war GDR building styles, the occasional nineteenth-century facade. But if one looks closely at the ground, one will see the rim of the foundation of what was Berlin's oldest synagogue, established in 1712 at Heidereuter-gasse 4. Until that time, only private synagogues were allowed. One might assume that the building was destroyed in *Kristallnacht*, but in fact it was an air raid that brought it to the ground, and a housing block was built over a portion of the lot in 1968 when the ruins could have been repaired. The last service took place here on 20 November 1942. I once had a student burst into tears here while examining the paltry foundations.

The street opposite the synagogue is also saturated with history and was the site of a protest by non-Jewish women petitioning for the release of their Jewish husbands. In February and March 1943 approximately five thousand protesters gathered in front of the detention centre located on Rosenstrasse. While the actions of the women were not directly responsible for freeing the men, the protest is nonetheless a remarkable instance of German civil disobedience, commemorated in 1995 with a 'Block der Frauen', or 'Women's Block', a monument planned in East German times, with a nearby sculpture of a Jewish man defying authority by sitting on a bench reserved for Aryans. The street seems to capture both the destruction of a community and its resilience.

The old Jewish quarter does not tell an encouraging story about the history of Jewish life in the city. Eighty per cent of Jews in the eighteenth century were very poor, and a smaller fraction were beggars (or *Betteljuden*); one can trace the evolution of the community as it enjoyed increasing wealth and integration into German society, and then experienced near destruction.

The Old Jewish Cemetery on Grosse Hamburger Strasse, in use until 1827, had almost three thousand graves and was

Kippot, at the entrance to a Jewish cemetery.

Ruins of the Jewish cemetery at Schönhauser Allee. This gravestone was shattered and blasted onto its side during bombing in the Second World War.

levelled by the SS with superstitious fury in 1943. It later became a mass grave for neighbourhood Germans who were killed in bombings, mixing the remains of the old Jewish graves with Second World War victims. There were Christian crosses here until the 1970s for lost family members, making this a complicated place of remembrance, until the space was restituted to the Jewish community, which erected a single symbolic gravestone, for the philosopher Moses Mendelssohn (1729–1786), made from many broken tombstones. The other important Jewish cemeteries are at Schönhauser Allee and in Weissensee – at the former, an air raid shattered the cemetery, so that now the entire space is a pile of broken tombstones consumed by moss and grass.

Next door on Grosse Hamburger Strasse at No. 27, the Jewish high school still has the pre-war inscription 'Jewish Boys School', despite being used as a deportation centre in 1942. From here, down Auguststrasse, one comes to locations that suggest the sophistication and successes of the German-Jewish community: the old Jewish hospital on Auguststrasse and the Hildesheimer Rabbinical Seminary (founded in 1873, closed in 1938 and now an Orthodox synagogue). Around the

Stolpersteine, or 'stumbling stones', commemorating the victims of National Socialism at their last place of residence.

corner, the domed New Synagogue on Oranienburger Strasse, built between 1859 and 1866 by the architect Edward Knoblauch, replaced the smaller Old Synagogue that we just visited. These and other Jewish institutions are now heavily guarded by police and barriers, as unsurprisingly the potential for a – one would hope, unlikely – anti-Semitic attack on a Jewish institution is taken very seriously given Berlin's history.

Throughout these streets, you might notice pieces of the world's largest monument, the *Stolpersteine*. Meaning 'stumbling stones', the idea is that passers-by in the streets of Berlin, and now many other European cities, trip over these slightly raised tiny bronze plaques fixed with a hammer drill and cement, not just physically, but intellectually. They record the last known residence of a victim of the Third Reich, their name, date of birth and the details of their deportation and where and how they were *ermordert*, 'murdered': the project does not mince words. Each stone measures 10 by 10 centimetres, and there are now 25 square kilometres of them in total. Gunter Demnig is the creator of the project, which started as an illegal initiative in 1997 in Berlin and was officialized by 2000 – one can imagine how difficult it would

The Jewish Museum, designed by architect Daniel Libeskind.

be in Germany to dig up a memorial to a Holocaust victim, although in Munich a citywide ban proved very embarrassing to the city. Demnig says: 'A man is first forgotten when his name is forgotten,' although what strikes me as most poignant about the monument is the insufficiency of the inscription to conjure a person. It is the emptiness, the void, the lack of more personalized information, the maw of the forgotten, which gives the monuments their power and lifts them from the banality of a statistic.

One of the most poignant *Stolpersteine* I know, perhaps because I have read about the family history, is in front of a café in a building that belonged to a Jewish family. Café Einstein's Stammhaus, on Kurfürstenstrasse 58, is an old villa, one of a few lone survivors in a part of the Schöneberg that is windy and full of wide avenues. Some deride the café's efforts to be a Viennese coffeehouse – with excellent Wiener Schnitzel,

Apfelstrudel and Wiener Melange coffee – in the more Spartan northern capital. But the way the past is dealt with here is decidedly more German than Austrian. The *Stolpersteine* outside indicate that the owners were the Blumenfelds. Margarete and Georg bought the house in the 1920s and opened a casino here in 1932. The couple committed suicide, a 'dignified exit', Georg in 1938, two years before his wife. Upstairs lived the silent film actress Henny Porten, whose career had ended not only with the introduction of sound in cinema, but as a result of the policies of Joseph Goebbels, because she was married to a Jewish doctor. She died impoverished in 1960.

Of course, places of Jewish remembrance are found throughout the city. A short walk from the Brandenburg Gate, memorials are tucked into a corner of the Tiergarten, because they are close to the centres of government control. At one time, Prussian palaces along the Wilhelmstrasse had ministerial gardens that stretched out towards the park, and a section of this historic green space was given to the Memorial to the Murdered Jews of Europe.

The Memorial has been in a constant state of debate, even since its opening. The 2,711 steles of the memorial on a massive city block are an enormous admission of state guilt. Finished in 2004, and designed by the American-Jewish architect Peter Eisenman, the Memorial cost €25 million. Walking, descending, through the space is a disorienting experience: the ground rises and falls, the steles are rarely at perfect right angles. At the eastern end of the installation, underground, is an information centre that contains the names of all the known victims of the Shoah, documented at the Holocaust Museum at Yad Vashem near Jerusalem.

But the Jewish community was not entirely pleased with the space. One of the major scandals involved the use of an anti-graffiti protectant on the steles, produced by Degussa, which, with its subsidiary Degesch, and IG Farben, was responsible for the production of the Zyklon-B insecticide used to gas victims in the Nazi death camps. The state did not spend the €3 million it would have cost to reverse the mistake. Also, the memorial is subject to the criticism that only Jews are memorialized here, and many feel that one should think more broadly about the Nazis' victims, and not play the game of identity politics – across the street is the Memorial to Persecuted Homosexuals, and closer to the Reichstag the Memorial to Murdered Sinti and Roma. This atomizing of victimhood, however, was a response to the first gesture of the state post-reunification in 1993 to memorialize all victims of war and tyranny at the Neue Wache. The Old Prussian guardhouse (1818) on Unter den Linden contains an aggrandized (and quite Christian) *pietà* sculpture by Käthe Kollwitz, and many feel that it is a place where both fallen Nazi soldiers and their Jewish victims are remembered. Whether the Memorial to the Murdered Jews is too abstract, and could be mistaken for a memorial to the Berlin Wall – or whether it is misused by visitors who play hide and seek in its forest of steles, or climb on top of them laughing and jumping, or use them as a striking background for selfies on social media, such as Grindr – are issues of concern. The space nonetheless is a prominent and poignant part of the Berlin cityscape.

Walking distance south is one of Berlin's most celebrated buildings, commissioned in 1989 and completed in 1999 to 'deal with the fundamental question of Jewish participation in the history of Berlin': the Jewish Museum. The most striking aspect of the place is the architecture of the Polish-American-Jewish architect Daniel Libeskind, to the extent that some have argued that it is a piece of sculpture that stands on its own, overpowering the much less distinguished, and quite small, collection that previously occupied just a few rooms on Oranienburger Strasse. That said, the building itself – a weathered zinc zigzag with razor edges that has oxidized and turned blue over time – is in the form of a shattered Star of David, with voids (a disquieting Holocaust Tower that allows in only a shard of light, or a Garden of Exile where olive trees are immobilized by cement). However, in this narrative of rupture, the interior exhibition space creates continuities, axes representing Exile and the Holocaust that eventually lead to the exhibits. The building is connected to a more distant past through the museum's entrance in the 1734–5 Kollegienhaus. I think that the criticism that the collection cannot live up to the space does not do enough justice to the building itself being an expression of the continuities and discontinuities of more than two thousand years of German-Jewish history. The museum frequently hosts exhibits on contemporary Jewish life in Berlin, and it is worth noting that Berlin now has the fastest-growing Jewish population in Germany, perhaps in Europe. The old institutions are being brought back to life. In fact, the continuities of Jewish life in Berlin suggested in Libeskind's building may ultimately prove to be stronger than anyone could foretell.

One sees this growth in the statistics. The massive influx of Israelis has come precisely because many have a strong cultural connection to Germany – their grandparents spoke Yiddish, they grew up with Central European cuisine, their intellectual and musical culture was Benjamin and Bach. Many come on German passports issued because their ancestors fled the country. Three thousand new passports are issued to Israelis each year, and over 100,000 have already successfully applied for and received them. Angela Merkel, on a state visit to Israel in February 2014, announced a bilateral deal that allows Israelis between the ages of eighteen and thirty to work in Germany. As one friend from Haifa told me, 'It's more dangerous to be a Jew these days in Israel than in Germany. Where would you rather raise your children? It's also a better place to be an artist.'

Determining the number of Jews in Berlin is difficult, as so many are secular, and census data is based on nationality and not on religion (which leads to a conflation of Israeli with Jew), unless you are paying the dreaded Church Tax to either the Evangelical or Catholic communities. One can, however, make an estimate. According to the Israeli Embassy, approximately twenty thousand Israelis live in Berlin, officially, but the unofficial number is much higher because not all of them are registered. More than ten thousand people are registered as members of the city's Jewish community, according to the Jüdische Gemeinde zu Berlin, making it the largest Jewish

The Memorial to the Murdered Jews of Europe, opened in 2005.

religious community in Germany. But again, this is not indicative, as many residents are secular. The German civil authorities note that fifteen thousand Israelis come to live in Germany every year and even though ten thousand find their way back to Israel again, five thousand remain. With up to six daily flights between Israel and the German capital – you can even fly budget on easyJet – tourism from Israel to Berlin increased sixfold just between 2010 and 2012, leading to many longer stays. Based on this information, the press estimates the number of Jews living in Berlin at fifty thousand, an increase of more than 800 per cent since 1990, and these numbers are set to grow. In 1933, 160,000 Jews lived here, and so one might optimistically say that Berlin is well on its way to replenishing that number, reduced by exile and mass murder.

I recently attended an alternative Shabbas ceremony popular with the Israeli queer community, called 'Let's Start Davening'. The cantor flies in from Tel Aviv and leads the recitation of prayers for Kabbalat Shabbat, or the ceremony to receive the holy Friday eve. The crowd is not simply composed of gay expat Israelis, but also families with children, old Berlin Jews and curious young people of all faiths. An Israeli artist who has lived in Berlin for five years turns to me and he says, 'In Israel this wouldn't work: there wouldn't be this mix of people. It would be stiffer and more self-conscious, especially among the gay men.' The evening is remarkably inclusive in yet another way: I was not asked once whether I was Jewish. On our way out, the men debate how much they liked the evening – for many it was their first time, 'LSD virgins', as they put it. One says, 'It's beautiful: it's the way all religion should be: queer, open, accepting. This is the model for Judaism.' Another says, 'I'd have preferred to be home, reading Christopher Hitchens.' Three of them then discuss whether any of them would go back to Israel, and not one says yes.

Is this an answer to the young woman who asked me how one can live in this city, walk down these streets, pass so many monuments to the dead, aware of the incalculable loss? If Berlin, of all places, can prove that Jews, secular or not, are safe here, then I can answer yes.

Underground

Like Paris, Edinburgh or Naples, Berlin is a double city, whose underground tunnels and bunkers are by now mythological. The most compelling recesses are neither ancient sewer systems nor catacombs, but rather more recent public works: the mass transportation system and the shelters built for wartime.

The underground train system or U-Bahn, *Untergrundbahn*, is run by the BVG (*Berliner Verkehrsbetriebe*), while the rapid transit S-Bahn is run by Deutsche Bahn. This has recently made the S-Bahn more susceptible to strikes – a source of ire for Berliners used to estimating their commute by the minute. While the U-Bahn is a slower, local, underground train (80 per cent below the city's surface), the S-Bahn is a faster, mostly overground train connecting the eastern and western edges of the city – Ostkreuz to Westkreuz, for example – in 28 minutes.

The Berlin U-Bahn is one of the great metro systems of the world, with half a billion yearly passengers, ten lines, 173 stations and 150 km of track. The S-Bahn is even more extensive, with about as many stations but more than twice as much track. Like its counterparts in other European capitals, the transport system has its iconic characteristics. I would not say one of them is the smell (faintly rubbery, perhaps from brakes), as in Paris with its marked metallic or sulphurous odour. Nor is the Berliner U-Bahn particularly deep or claustrophobic, with low-ceilinged cars, as in London. Berlin's runs shallow, an underground train rather than a tube.

When people think of Berlin's transport system, there are other iconic sensory cues. The pattern of the U-Bahn seats – which resembles a colour-blindness test in blue, white, black and red – must be one of the ugliest in the world. Or they think of the ubiquitous yellow branding of the BVG. Or the plain-clothes ticket controllers, sometimes mistaken for homeless people, with deep back pockets to conceal their sophisticated machines to print your fine. But most of all, the S-Bahn is symbolized by the rising and falling major third when the metro doors close, a sound that was sampled by the Berlin DJ Paul Kalkbrenner for his film *Berlin Calling* and its electronic soundtrack to great effect.

A New Yorker in Berlin will be impressed by how often trains run, 24 hours on Friday and Saturdays – and the reassuring countdown of minutes to the next departure. And by the honour system: there are no turnstiles, which means there are also no impediments to big bags or convoluted tunnels to keep those with tickets separate from those without. But our New Yorker might be perturbed by the silence that reigns on most journeys compared to the spirited public spectacles on the L train to Brooklyn. That is, except when the Berlin party set crowd the U1 at midnight, or the U8 – the so-called *Achterbahn*, or 'roller coaster' – drinking from their Berliner Pilsners, already starting the party (walking Berlin with an open beer in your hand is a pleasure, of course, denied North Americans at home). Or when there's a revolving party on the Circle Line, or *Ringbahn*, with no end station, until the police break things up, citing noise rules and selectively enforcing the recent but still lax laws about alcohol on board.

But with the everyday silence, one notices too that others don't seem to pay you much attention, something peculiar about Berlin that gives visitors a sense of freedom. The democratic dress sense of the U-Bahn is accentuated by the fact that you are more likely to see your government official with briefcase and splattered house painter sitting side by side here than in, say, Paris. If anything, there is a pressure on certain U-Bahn lines to dress down. A lawyer friend, who recently moved, complained that the U8 line was so much grubbier than her former stretch of the U6 between expensive Mitte and western Kreuzberg: 'I don't know how comfortable I'll feel in my business suit coming home in the evenings.

I might have to get my bike fixed.' But, on the other hand, if you were to ride the U-Bahn in your housecoat, no one would allow themselves to bat an eye. Meanwhile, public transport is often faster and more convenient than driving a car and finding parking, which means it keeps city traffic quiet except for the fleets of cyclists using the city's ubiquitous dedicated biking lanes.

The Berlin underground is also a place for artistic experimentation: Mozart operas have been performed in unfinished stations, and one finds plenty of innovative street art. But for many the most intriguing art exhibits are the typefaces of the U-Bahn's many station signs. In general, as elsewhere in Germany, the Antiqua fonts have a starkness and sharp edge that distinguish them from the more humanist but corporate Johnston sans serif of the London Underground. But this is a generalization: Berlin's underground typefaces on station signs are not standardized as they are in many cities. There are hobbyists here who are expert at dating station signs by their fonts. The stripped-down sans-serif modernist typeface along the U8 line, known as Neuzeit Grotesk, can be dated to the First World War, and the bubbly Octopuss font of Pankstrasse to 1977. The north–south S-Bahn line, built in the 1930s, features the difficult-to-read broken Fraktur (or Gothic) black letter script erroneously associated with the Nazis, who, in fact, banned it in 1941. The U-Bahn and S-Bahn plan also offers an

Going underground into the Berlin U-Bahn.

intriguing graphic universe. It is less of an abstraction of the reality above ground than in London. But its elegant yet intricate rationalization gives the impression of a mega-city rather than the ragged disjointedness of many *Kieze*, and the empty spaces between, above ground.

S-Bahn and U-Bahn tunnels were terrifying places in the endgame of the Second World War. They were used by soldiers of both sides. Thousands hid in them during the battle above ground, and many were injured. There is some debate on the matter, but it is most likely that it was only on the eve of defeat, on 2 May 1945, that the SS detonated the section of S-Bahn tunnel passing under the Landwehrkanal, flooding the U-Bahn system all over Berlin, to drown enemy troops. The U-Bahn was only pumped out six months later. Flak towers were another location of wartime suffering: multi-level installations of reinforced concrete with a cellar floor, built as protection from Allied bombing. The tower at Humboldthain, in Wedding, was only partly destroyed by the French occupying forces, and because it was buried in 1.5 million cubic metres of rubble, it is now a remarkable underground gallery of dripping stairwells and forlorn spaces maintained by the Berlin Underground Society, who also care for the numerous Second World War bunkers and tunnels around the city.

With the city's division, the U-Bahn and S-Bahn were divided between East and West. The S-Bahn, along with waterways, was operated by the East Germans until 1984, and before then subject to boycott. Well after reunification, the former East German carriages with their creaky wooden seats were a novelty reminder of the old system on the East–West route. The U-Bahn meanwhile was shared between East and West, creating some of the Berlin Wall's most intriguing spaces. U-Bahn lines that originated and ended in the West, even though they passed under East German territory, remained in Western hands. This meant passengers on Western lines, after the Berlin Wall went up, would in fact pass through abandoned East German 'ghost stations' before emerging back in the West. Portcullis devices would rise and fall to let the Western trains enter the East, to prevent underground

In the U-Bahn, with its famous seat pattern.

escapes, while East German guards patrolled the otherwise empty train platforms. Because track maintenance was the responsibility of the East, and substandard, West German trains risked breaking down en route under East German territory. When the Wall finally came down, the many ghost stations, on the U8 and U6 lines, for example, proved to be time capsules of advertisements from 1961. The stations were simply refurbished and reopened: it is remarkable how easily the network was stitched back together.

It was the Friedrichstrasse Station U-Bahn and S-Bahn interchange in East Berlin that came to be a symbol of the division of the country. The station, built in 1878, gained its elegant halls and dark glass shed in the 1920s. Having survived the Second World War, it became the main traffic juncture between the Eastern and Western zones, and the location of most of the human flight from East to West before 1961. The East German author Claudia Rusch once told me that she only came to understand what had been done to her country when she was allowed to see the entirety of the station after *Die Wende*. Here was the logic of the Berlin Wall under one roof: all those many places an Easterner had not been allowed to see, resulting in an incomplete understanding of the total space, and curious compensations to have it make sense. The station had been a terrifying maze of guard dogs, partitions, camera surveillance, multiple passport and customs checks and interrogations, accompanied by the grotesque project of amassing hard currency through mandatory money exchanges and the sale to Westerners of products unavailable to the East's own citizens. It was also a place of considerable intrigue, with special escape and entry–exit routes for double agents to the West. Overshadowing all these mechanizations was the human tragedy: the exit hall, through which those departing to the West would leave their families behind, came to be known for obvious and painful reasons as the 'Palace of Tears'.

Sexuality City

On Nollendorfstrasse, at number 17, you might want to stand and whistle up to the window and see if anyone opens it.

> And soon the whistling will begin. Young men are calling to their girls. Standing down there in the cold, they whistle up at the lighted windows of warm rooms where the beds are already turned down for the night. They want to be let in.

I tried this once, passing through this Schöneberg street one evening, and someone did open the window, but she looked as though she might call the police. Not that I really expected Christopher Isherwood, peeking through his blinds, to open the window of the apartment where he once lived, surprised because he had thought that the whistling 'could not possibly be – for me'.

While homosexuality was still illegal in Berlin in the 1920s, the infamous Paragraph 175 was not enforced, and Isherwood, along with his poet friends W. H. Auden and Stephen Spender, could indulge in proclivities that were strictly forbidden back home in Britain. As Isherwood wrote, 'It was Berlin itself he was hungry to meet . . . to Christopher, Berlin meant Boys.' Many of the homosexual bars that they frequented were located around this *Kiez* in Schöneberg, including the Eldorado transvestite club (which he calls the Alexander Casino in his writings), which was shut down by the Nazis and is now an organic food market. These days the neighbourhood around Nollendorfplatz, and especially down Motzstrasse, is adorned

Berlin's bar scene: Rauschgold in Kreuzberg.

with rainbow flags and dotted with leather shops, bars and establishments with dodgy happenings in the basements.

Schöneberg is stereotyped as catering for mature gay men. Many of the neighbouring bars have clienteles rather older than fifty. Certainly much of West Berlin's gay history happened here. The terror of the Nazi years was followed by the enforcement of Paragraph 175 in West Germany until 1969; it was only fully scrapped in 1994. Schöneberg in the 1970s and '80s became a gay centre once again, as it had been in the 1920s. Much of the current scene feels like a leftover from thirty years ago.

But this is not entirely fair, and curious tourists looking for 'Berlin's gay village' can find in certain establishments a well-scrubbed, pretty, young and entirely male public. Here you can order a skinny pink cocktail decorated with fruit and umbrella, sit on a cheetah-skin sofa, and spend the evening mouthing Madonna lyrics. One can enjoy gay life as packaged by the gay magazines. The other public well catered for is the leather scene. Germany's long tradition of artisanal leatherwork finds expression in the number of fetish shops on Fuggerstrasse, which do intricate tailor-made work, also in rubber and latex.

While I am glad Schöneberg exists, it is not where I prefer to spend my time. Some spurious statistic not worth footnoting estimates that Berlin has the highest gay population in Europe. Berlin had a gay mayor, Klaus Wowereit, from 2001 to 2014, known for his clever one-liners, such as 'I am gay, and it's also good that way' (*Ich bin schwul, und das ist auch gut so*). The point is that it is hardly an environment where one needs to go looking for a 'gay village', when the whole city is a ghetto.

Since reunification, the bar scene has moved further east into first Prenzlauer Berg and Mitte, and now, increasingly, Kreuzberg and Neukölln, where the crowds are noticeably more mixed in gender and self-definition. Outside of Silver Future, in Neukölln, the queer crowd, mostly lesbian, but also gay and trans, or non-defining, sits under an inventive art exhibit. The soundtrack is electronic; there are zines about theoretical sexualities lying around. There is no dress code, although the aesthetic might be called glam-industrial. In nearby Kreuzberg, much of the scene is multicultural in character – be it at the community-oriented Südblock, or the monthly party, Gayhane, for the gay Turkish and Arabic community. Many come to Berlin expecting blond beasts, but here the choice is rather more varied. In Roses, one of my favourite hangouts in this neighbourhood, the crowd is remarkably international and mixed gay–straight. The space is entirely covered with pink faux fur on the inside,

The Möbel Olfe bar in Kreuzberg, located in a former furniture shop.

and religious icons. It is a little like being inside a Muppet's vagina. In general, these scenes cater to a mixed-age public, with as many twenty- as forty-year-olds, and they reject the body culture and labels of commercialized 'gay' culture.

It would be a mistake to dismiss Schöneberg, however, even if Neukölln-Kreuzberg is more your cup of tea. It must be said that the latter's polysexual, mixed-gender community is indebted to the more homogeneous community of Schöneberg for their fight for liberation and rights in the 1980s – a rights movement that remains unfinished and requires solidarity, not antipathies. Despite all of this local acceptance, today in Germany there is still no gay marriage or adoption, and the fight has been left unfinished. This story is well documented in exhibits at Berlin's Schwules Museum, or 'Gay Museum', located north of Nollendorfplatz. The museum is the successor in many senses to the infamous Institute of Sexual Science of Magnus Hirschfeld, and the long history of sexual research and political organization which made Berlin the birthplace of the gay liberation movement as early as the 1850s, and which suffered such a tragic history in the twentieth century.

Now, how to meet a Berliner?

Simply whistling is not quite enough these days. But doing much more can also be dangerous. A surprise for many visitors, gay and straight alike, is the amount of personal space that Berliners take, and how little value is placed on small talk. A *Madrileño* might feel all his social skills are wasted in Berlin. He's better off simply sitting on his hands and calibrating how close he's standing. 'Distance and respect' is the mantra. Endless questions and being chatty are the marks of superficiality, or a dangerous sign that you might continue the annoying banter between the sheets. Berlin is famous as the city – at least on the gay scene (many heterosexuals find it difficult to get past even the initial standoffishness) – where most of the conversation happens after sex. An aggressive look might be the only necessary prelude before something expected happens to you in a dark room, after which you might be permitted to inquire about someone's name, and maybe even get a phone number. This process is disheartening for romantics, those who rely on their witty conversation to get some, or those who need to feel a little more comfortable than being pressed against a cement wall.

Equally perplexing is the premium on honesty. In California I've witnessed the ubiquitous 'it was great, thanks' as a response to the waiter after a putrescent meal. This would never happen in Berlin. Likewise in the bar, Berliners regularly comment how unattractive they find one other, without taking it necessarily as an insult. Rather, why waste time? In the case of attraction, visitors on the gay scene might be surprised by how straightforward locals can be, and how quickly things can turn into sex. The fact that Berlin has low levels of criminality also dispenses with the sex hotel culture that has evolved in, say, cities like Rio – you are more likely to end up at someone's house and have him make you breakfast.

Perhaps because Berlin is one of the most secular (godless?) places on the planet, there is a low social cost from being promiscuous or going to a sex club; there's no pretending that you are a good girl, no need to hide your adventures from your friends. An open relationship (a 'Berlin relationship', as some call it) is the norm rather than the exception. I have plenty of gay friends who feel oppressed in the city, judged harshly as 'conservative' because they are in monogamous relationships. Others complain that Berlin is a revolving door of talent, making it hard to have any kind of relationship, because something better always seems to come along.

Berlin is not 'conservative'. In the basement of that power plant turned nightclub, Berghain, is the city's most famous gay sex club, with nights appealing to a revealing number of fetishes from latex, to scat and piss, to formal and office dress. I've heard that at 'Office Slut' the action happens on photocopiers. The same level of sexual liberty goes for women, which means that they arguably have better agency over their sexuality in a society unlikely to shame them. The lesbian scene, while relatively not as sex-driven as the gay sex clubs, has a reputation for being less competitive than in other cities. The trans community has events as diverse as literary salons and the yearly ironic 'Tranny [sic] Olympics'.

For heterosexuals, the KitKatClub, the name of the space in the Isherwoodian *Cabaret*, is a massive burlesque palace with hundreds of heterosexual couples writhing downstairs in the Dragon Room, while on the dance floor upstairs a polysexual 'sex dance' takes place. Meanwhile, swingers' clubs and private parties for straight or polysexual couples are popular. Many establishments have dress codes: I can think of one with a 1920s flapper casino theme – you can imagine what is being gambled. All this leaves out the labyrinthine online world – of dating, hook-ups, BDSM and the like – which seem less important than in cities where it is more expensive to go out.

Berlin's bar scene is not only frequented by nubile youth. Many people in their thirties, forties, fifties or older come to Berlin and find that staying up late at night is not just for twenty-year-olds, and that being in the city has them acting like teenagers a decade or two longer than they expected. All this can have a deleterious effect on good judgement and personal health. In the 1990s, Amsterdam was the city overzealous parents wouldn't let their kids travel to because of the drugs. Today, it must be Berlin because of the sex.

Sex work is meanwhile legal in Berlin; workers charge VAT and pay taxes in advance based on predicted yearly income. Kurfürstenstrasse, not far from Café Einstein, is commonly perceived as one of Berlin's more downmarket prostitution *Striche* or catwalks, with pornography shops, empty lots, some high-end furniture shops, immigrant-owned vegetable markets and rent-boy bars. I recently met a property owner intent on opening a love hotel on this strip, because he said charging by the hour was rather more lucrative than making money on monthly rent. A more touristic version of the same *Strich* is on Oranienburger Strasse, while many search online or at one of the city's many 'wellness brothel establishments'. One prominent space includes a 'bio-sauna', a restaurant with 'leisurely breakfasts', and of course, if you 'feel like more', there's an extra fee for a half-hour of 'excellent sex' in one of the 'love suites . . . individually decorated with wall to wall paintings by professional artists'.

Demonstration in Neukölln supporting gay Muslims in Berlin.

Some of the questions I get asked are: why are Berliners not uptight about sex? Why do they have so many fetishes? Or are fetishes substitutes for being uptight? Does it have something to do with the easy-going attitude to nudity? It's hard to be conclusive, but Berlin certainly does have a different ethos from the 'Anglo-Saxon' capitals. As the London–Berlin performance artist La JohnJoseph put it in an interview:

> I find sexuality to be very fluid here, much more than London, where people are really uptight about sex and sexuality. Here you can have nudity without it being pornographic or prudish. In America, nudity is always pornographic and in England it is always prudish. And I think that really informs sexuality. I also think people have the time in this city to have a sexuality. In London, you don't have time to have a sexuality. In London, you have your 'economically viable' relationship whether you like it or not.

If you go to any Berlin lake, you will find whole families getting naked together on the public beach without a second thought. The traditional sauna culture in the city is usually mixed-sex, often including the changing facilities, and entirely FKK, *Freikörperkultur* (Free Body Culture), or nudist. These spaces are not particularly sexual in character. Berliners at the elegant and relaxing 'textile-free' Vabali spa simply aren't paying attention to the fact that you are sitting naked in a pool with twenty other people of all ages, weights and genders. This lack of concern about nudity may take away a level of shame and anxiety about the body and its imperfections.

In looking for reasons why Berliners are more relaxed about sex, one might point to the city's proletarian roots, the low levels of bourgeois propriety, its secular rejection of Protestantism, but all this might be simplifying. Perhaps a city that has seen so much destruction of the human body might have good reason to celebrate it.

I Heart Kotti

On a summer's night, walk through Mariannenplatz and its *chiaroscuro* montage, of trees in half shadow, uplit partially by an illuminated brick wall, a pastiche of graffiti. The gloom should somehow be silent and empty, but it is darted with activity. Under the pools of light from the park's lanterns sit young people in circles on unkempt grass listening to a guitar and drinking brew they've bought from a *Späti*, or night shop. Bikes glide through the frieze, towards the evening buzz of Oranienstrasse, the *Kiez* of 'SO36', and then the canal where the lights of restaurants are a sinewy chain along the darkened channel. Couples sit close in the warm air between the bankside greenery, their legs dangling into the obscurity. There's another bright cling of a cyclist's bell, the hum of distant traffic, some laughter, and then the sudden beat of swans' wings under the bridges. In such a humming place in the city's heart, where you find its most varied street life, so many overgrown corners would be brightly illuminated for safety somewhere else; but here to do so would be a little like turning on the bright lights on a high school dance.

The overground U1 line is an illuminated spectacle, a bright phantom, suited in the BVG's yellow colour, passing above the darkened street life, and pulls in at Kottbusser Tor, or 'Kotti' as the neighbours affectionately call the ramshackle roundabout. Looming is the building some call 'the monster'. It is Brutalist, ten storeys high, and it hulks over the square. It's stained with water and studded with satellite dishes. More than a thousand people live inside it, mostly immigrant families from Eastern Anatolia, who came to Germany with the guest worker

The erstwhile punk neighbourhood of SO36, in former West Berlin.

programme. The Neues Kreuzberger Zentrum (NKZ), finished in 1974, is their beast. But it's a beloved animal.

Architects exert themselves designing attractive public spaces, but they cannot easily predict use. The NKZ is for many people ugly: a brutal modernist housing block rising from the low-rise *Mietskasernen*. The single building was the subject recently of an international symposium on 'failed architecture'. But its makeshift quality, its shabbiness, makes the NKZ unthreatening, organic, comfortable, disarming and spontaneous. It is popular with hipsters, perhaps, because they ironize the 'ugly' space. The massive housing estate is eaten away, on the ground and first floors, by a motley mix of kebab stands, old-man shisha parlours, betting offices and queer bars. A city street of beeping vehicles passes through an arch in the middle. On one corner, addicts with their dogs loiter. Businesses front the upstairs balconies – there is a safe space for transsexuals, a meeting place for leftist activists – and down below Turkish-German families and veiled women pass through the shabby alley and interior passageways, giving the place the Orientalized atmosphere of a small souk. At night, the NKZ has many dark corners, and in the 1980s these were popular with heroin addicts, but they have been mostly pushed out. Recently, they have been replaced by petty thieves and drug pushers – the subject of plenty of media attention – but Kotti remains relatively safe compared to 'problem' neighbourhoods in most other European capitals.

A young man approaches and sits down right next to me on the steps leading up to the second level: more often than not the standard German rules of giving strangers 'distance and respect' are suspended here. Murat is wearing Adidas tracksuit trousers, trainers, a white vest and an oversized baseball cap. I half expect to be propositioned. We chit-chat and I ask him if the bar flooded with ungrateful fluorescent light, where the patriarchs are playing backgammon, tolerates its neighbour, an industrial gay bar in a former furniture shop. He shrugs and says, pointing to one establishment, 'Of course. They're all men in there,' and then pointing to the other, 'And all men in there too.' Laughing, he adds, 'No one cares what you do here. You're in Kotti.'

And I believe what he says. Or, at least, that they tolerate one another. The difficult task, however, is for a young man named Murat to find that tolerance elsewhere. In the shabby and economically depressed alleys of Kotti, almost everyone

The Neues Kreuzberger Zentrum (NKZ) is a modernist housing project in Kreuzberg, finished in 1974.

Döner is the street food invented in Kreuzberg.

is treated like a local. But the moment you leave, you are the underclass who comes from that place called Kotti.

Kreuzberg contains the largest Turkish diaspora community in the world. And, once a peripheral part of West Berlin which attracted punks and immigrants, it found itself right up against the historic centre of Mitte when the Wall fell. Investment has poured in, putting pressure on marginalized communities and those on social benefits. Plenty of asylum seekers from Africa are located here as well, with the police in recent conflict with those forced into the drug trade in local Görlitzer Park (a long and sad story). Rental prices are one area of great concern, with property prices affected by rising tourist numbers and wealthy gentrifiers.

In front of Südblock, a scrappy queer community *Biergarten* on the corner under the U-Bahn tracks, is a small hut with an 'I Heart Kotti' sign on it. Walk in at most times of day, and you will find groups of veiled teenagers, their parents and local punkish activists. I talk to a young Turkish-German man, in a carefully ironed white shirt, who tells me just how much rental prices are increasing in this part of former West Berlin, and how these are threatening the unique balance of people who live here. 'If immigrant families, who have lived here for almost three generations, are forced out from the place where they have their community, and into cheaper housing somewhere at the end of the S-Bahn line, where no one has ever seen an immigrant before, what do you expect will happen? We have created something special in Kreuzberg that is under threat.' Gentrification here is intimately connected to the question of whether Kotti will remain an example of diversity – of what is possible, in terms of tolerance in an increasingly xenophobic and frightened Europe.

Kreuzberg's popularity today is, of course, bound up with the unusual hybrid of Turkish and Arabic immigrant commerce, counterculture institutions and the new foodie and trendy culture brought by more recent arrivals. One of the best examples of the latter is Markthalle 9. While down the Landwehrkanal twice a week a massive 'Turkish' market occupies the length of the bank of the Maybachufer, on many days of the week another market takes place on Eisenbahnstrasse. It is called 'Number 9' because there were fourteen such neighbourhood market spaces created in Berlin in the late nineteenth century. Most have been remodelled, some occupied by soulless chain supermarkets, others into relatively antiseptic but still lovely market spaces (such as 'Number 12', the Marheineke Markthalle on Bergmannstrasse). 'Number 9' is creaky and unfinished inside, a survivor of the Kaiserreich era, except it has a low-rise Aldi supermarket occupying one corner. The high-raftered space was otherwise empty except for a couple of counters where one could order a beer. Then, in 2009, new plans for the space were drafted. Come here today on a Tuesday, Friday or Saturday, and the Markthalle 9 is buzzing with farmers from Spreewald in Brandenburg selling their seasonal produce; young Italians serving up fresh pasta, or pulled pork and other barbeque specialities that they fell in love with during an American stay; French, Austrian and Spanish cured meat and cheese stands; a canteen serving organic quinoa salads and daily plates; a coffee bar where the arabica grounds are meticulously weighed. On Thursday nights, the place is packed for a street

The popular Markthalle 9, a food market in Kreuzberg.

food evening, as are the monthly Sunday breakfast markets. It's all rather a step up from what normally poses as a local delicacy: Berliner currywurst, or processed sausage dressed in Allied rations (American ketchup, British India curry powder). Like many innovations by Kreuzberg's cosmopolitan young public, the Markthalle is something of a victim of its own success – on Thursdays it is hard to move your elbows as you try to eat *Fatteh* off a paper plate while standing. For some, it is the archetypal hipster-gentrification market, but for others it remains a relatively unvarnished success story of small-scale individual entrepreneurship. Whether the Martkhalle is simply a gentrification pioneer – as are also its cognates in the bar and restaurant scene elsewhere here and in Neukölln – that will lead inexorably to Covent Garden-style tourism, or, more likely, the arrival of a grand concern, like an Eataly replacing the Aldi, remains to be seen.

For those living in the *Bezirk* of Neukölln, a changing blue-collar borough of the former West, the area around Kotti, and

The Landwehr-Canal, which runs through Kreuzberg.

elsewhere in Kreuzberg, is already hopelessly gentrified. Property prices average well above €4,000 a square metre in Kreuzberg while you can still find apartments for half that in deepest Neukölln – but, mind you, these numbers are only indicative, as most people rent. This quarter is the edge of gentrification in today's Berlin, and the subject of endless public comment and policy. Once considered Berlin's 'dangerous neighbourhood', it is now an English-, Italian- and Spanish-speaking enclave. Brooklynites, east Londoners and Southern Europeans fleeing unemployment have flooded here for cheap rents, art spaces and alternative-scene nightlife. Walk through 'Kreuzkölln', that corner of the *Bezirk* closest to Kreuzberg along the canal, and one mostly hears English spoken.

The public reaction to gentrification has been trenchant and at times nasty: in Neukölln's Schillerkiez, not far from Boddinstrasse U8, natives have reacted with 'neighbourhood patrols' (*Kiez-Patrouille*) accompanied by angry dogs asking for the IDs of people who look too rich or foreign for the

'Kreuzberg remains unfriendly', written at the entrance to Markthalle 9.

neighbourhood. In Kreuzberg there have been 'anti-tourist' citizens' gatherings to deal with the invasion of their neighbourhood. *Touristenhass* ('hate of tourists') is of course xenophobia posing as social activism, the response of neighbourhoods unused to tourism being thrown into the big leagues (Berlin was the third most visited city in Europe last year, after Paris and London, at almost 30 million visits). At the level of the city, there have been more successful initiatives, such as a recent law for limiting sub-rentals and holiday apartments and the institution of universal rent control. Airbnb rentals and the like are seen to corrode neighbourhood life, flooding the quarter with a transient population, and causing a rise in apartment prices, as it is more lucrative to rent in the short rather than the long term. In 2014 the city responded with a law limiting new holiday flats and making two-thirds of the city's existing 18,000 vacation rentals illegal. In 2015 the city instituted its *Mietspreisbremse* (or rental break), meaning owners cannot charge more than 10 per cent higher than the average rental price in a neighbourhood for new rentals. After only one month, rental prices dropped 3 per cent across the city. The city is becoming a leader among capitals in fighting gentrification, with good public policy a more welcome approach than the neighbourhood mob mentality.

Nonetheless, Berlin is straining with change, and at times when I walk into the Markthalle 9, and see the graffito outside telling me *Kreuzberg bleibt unhöflich* ('Kreuzberg remains unfriendly'), I wonder about my neighbourhood. Am I yet another *arriviste* and unwelcome? The smiles I get from the Greek vendor selling goat feta and lentils with whom I talk regularly about the crisis; or the man at the French *épicerie* who gives his clients so many presents it should render his business unfeasible; or the neighbourhood old-timer at the key shop downstairs who should be a character in an Isherwood novel, whispering excitedly what she thinks is happening behind this or that locked door – they make me think that this unfriendly slogan, and others are, again, simple sass, or *Schnauze*. Or at least I hope so. Or are they a cry for help? Have I not left the 'old Kreuzberg' behind the moment I enter the 'new Kreuzberg' of the Markthalle, the gentrification pioneer? Kotti today – mixed-income and multicultural – has created one of the most diverse and creative neighbourhoods in Europe. The question is: for how long?

Forecourt at the Berlinische Galerie, the Yellow Field of Letters, by architects Kûhn Malvezzi.

Berlin 'Cool'

I am walking to a gritty industrial club, through the warehouses and parking lots of East Berlin's rust belt. I reach the darkened facade of a former factory alongside the tracks of Ostkreuz (where the local party scene has moved since the tourists discovered that 'super-club', Berghain). I clip around the building, take the back way, behind a pile of bricks or a broken wall of graffiti, past the fluorescent still-life of a security guard through a cubicle's window, past a vent that smells vaguely of poppers, until I hear voices as I turn the corner.

The line is long, and I chat with two British guys who drink Club Mate, a hipster stimulant, perhaps because they've also taken something that doesn't mix with alcohol. But they smell like *Döner* or perhaps *Gemüse Kebap*, so their stomachs are insulated for a good time. It's a summer night; the party's in the garden, the crowd heaving before the DJ. The moon is out, behind clouds; it's Caspar David Friedrich light. Or 'Prussian' blue, that eighteenth-century colour first invented in Berlin. I see the British dudes again; they're very friendly, one grabs me on the shoulder, buoyed by the pulsing electronica, the movement of lights, lifted by the warm air, the stars above, the diversity and happiness of the crowd, and he tells me: 'Amazing! This is Berlin!'

When I leave it is already day – one of those amazing Berlin June days that start the moment you walk out of the club in the early hours. I am saturated with cigarette smoke and sweat and kisses. The now faint blue above softens the steely train tracks. I go home, shower, sleep for a few hours, wake up for brunch with my friends. We compare our evening adventures – you never know what is going to happen to you when you

May Day demonstrations in Kreuzberg.

walk out of that door. We talk politics, sex and the news. The *New York Times* Styles section has been extolling again how much Brooklynites love Berlin, and the blogs have responded by saying that since Berlin's been 'discovered', it's now 'over'. Time to write the city's obituary because everyone's a tourist at Berghain! As a logical consequence, Berlin's 'no longer the coolest city in the world'.

We start discussing:

'Who moves to a city just because it's "cool"?'

'I know a few people here who did.'

'You're relevant just because you live in Berlin, didn't you know?'

'Better to say you're an artist in Berlin than unemployed and living at home in Bari.'

'Judging a whole city based on the popularity of a nightclub doesn't make any sense.'

'That's all people see when they come here, the city for them is a big nightclub.'

'Berlin's the best nightclub in the world!'

'Not any more, apparently.'

'They only see the *Technostrich* – '

'I don't even like riding my bike by there on a Saturday night.'

'How many of them you think have been to the Philharmonic?'

'I think Berlin would be happy to discover it's "over".'

'Over? Tell that to the Greeks. They'd be happy if Germany's star dimmed a little.'

'She means Berlin's over for the Peter Pans from Dalston.'

'What they see of Berlin is not even my weekend, let alone my week.'

It is perplexing the way the international press – *Rolling Stone, The Times, Vice* – weighs the status of Berlin's elusive 'cool' based on the fortunes of a nightclub, on whether the night-time itineraries of self-conscious club kids have been discovered by the masses. For those who actually live in the city, the dizzying array of concerts, clubs, festivals and street parties is just an awesome backdrop to the everyday. But otherwise it is hardly of consequence. What matters is that

Winter in Berlin. A view of a *Siedlung*, or social housing complex.

This rooftop bar, hidden on top of a sterile Neukölln shopping mall, is currently a darling of the international hipster crowd.

Berlin's still a place where people can pursue their creative work with fewer pressures from the market than in other European capitals, and have the opportunity to do so in an urbane international environment where they are allowed to live decently.

What would cause Berlin to be 'over'? If the conditions for its non-corporate lifestyle were suddenly to evaporate, there would be cause for concern. With property speculation and gentrification, this is the looming threat. But perhaps we have, after all, reasons to be optimistic. Despite the onslaught of gentrification, civic initiatives, such as rent control, are in place to protect the city's multi-income neighbourhoods, and there are some indications things will sooner get better than worse. Let's hope.

It would be wrong to say that optimism is a peculiarly Berlin perspective, as Berliners love to *meckern*, or complain. Perhaps for too long it was incomprehensible to believe that anything German could be 'cool'. I sometimes think these Berliners don't always appreciate what an outstanding city they have. Berlin will be tested in the years ahead as Europe confronts rising populism, nationalism, security concerns regarding terrorism, and the uncertainties of Trump's foreign policy. But things here are, especially in the longer view of the metropolis's history, better. The city remains in many ways a provincial place, one that has not yet reconciled

Hipsters on their laptops in the Sankt Oberholz café in Berlin-Mitte.

Friedrichshain's RAW Gelände, party spaces in an industrial park.

itself entirely to diversity, or the recent influx of creative folk. And yet, against the backdrop of what is Europe's foulest history, Berlin has left behind the worst – militarism, chauvinism and murderous state racism – and emerged democratic and egalitarian, full of great institutions, for the most part welcoming refugees, taking the best of preceding eras – tolerance, historical mindfulness and creative and intellectual dynamism. Berlin now needs to harness these achievements as we face an uncertain future.

Now, if we could only do something about those short, dark winter days. But then you bundle yourself against the wind, put on your headphones and send sparks down the cold of the S-Bahn tracks with an electronic soundtrack, light candles in the windows, and count out the hours with strong dark coffee and good conversation – and in Berlin there is plenty. Meanwhile, in summer, you don't need to do much more than buy a bottle of cold Pilsner, ride your bike down the blooming canal bank – past where the Turkish-German families are grilling, the Kreuzbergers are playing *boules*, locals are loitering at the tables in front of the *Späti* – to the Admiralbrücke. There, you can sit with your back to the water, watch the street hum with love, and observe how on this beautiful bright night, as the Berliners put it, 'everything's in butter' – *na, allet in Butta.*

The East Side Gallery's most iconic mural is Dmitri Vrubel's *Fraternal Kiss* (1990), picturing Leonid Brezhnev and Erich Honecker embracing in 1979 on the occasion of the GDR's 30th anniversary. More than a hundred murals adorn this kilometre stretch of the former Berlin Wall.

LISTINGS

MUSEUMS AND SITES

Museum Island

Mitte
www.smb.museum

Berlin's answer to the Louvre, this UNESCO world heritage site is an ensemble of five museums located along the Spree, including the **Pergamonmuseum** (archaeology, including the Ishtar Gate of Babylon and the Pergamon Altar; partially closed for refurbishment until 2019); the **Neues Museum** (early history and Egyptian collections including the Nefertiti Bust, in a remarkably poignant building that preserves Second World War damage); the **Alte Nationalgalerie** (Old National Gallery, of nineteenth-century art); the **Bode-Museum** (sculpture collections); and the **Altes Museum** (the first museum of the Island, with classical art). Buying a combination ticket is a good investment. Also on the island are the squat **Berlin Cathedral** and the **Berlin City Palace** (being rebuilt to open in 2019), which are not far from the **Nikolaiviertel** (the medieval 'old town' rebuilt by the East Germans in the 1980s).

Unter den Linden

Mitte

'Under the Linden Trees' is Berlin's most famous avenue, and one can walk from the Museum Island past the **German Historical Museum** in the 1706 Arsenal, to the **Brandenburg Gate**, with a detour via the elegant **Gendarmenmarkt** (a few streets south). The **Staatsoper** (State Opera House)**, Neue Wache** memorial to victims of war and tyranny, Bebelplatz **Memorial to the 1933 Book Burning** and **Humboldt University** are all located on this elegant boulevard.

Reichstag

Platz der Republik 1, Tiergarten
www.bundestag.de

The German Bundestag, or Parliament, is located under the dome, opened in 1999, designed by the architect Norman Foster, whose roof terrace can be visited by pre-registering online. A stunning

360° view can be enjoyed over the city and the **Tiergarten**, very much also worth visiting for its woods, small lakes, beer gardens (such as the Café am Neuen See), **Siegessäule** victory column and **Berlin Zoo.** A boat trip on the Spree from near the House of World Cultures is surprisingly delightful.

Kulturforum

Matthäikirchplatz, Tiergarten
www.smb.museum

On the edge of the Tiergarten near corporate Potsdamer Platz is the **Kulturforum** with its Old Masters' Gallery (**Gemäldegalerie**). The complex has one of Europe's most important collections of European painting from the thirteenth to eighteenth centuries, including works by Bruegel, Dürer, Giotto and Titian. One side of the gallery is dedicated to masters from the Flemish and German world, and the other to Southern Europe. A short walk from here is the modern art collection of the **Neue Nationalgalerie** (closed until 2019, but worth viewing from the outside), an elegant Mies van der Rohe glass pavilion. For contemporary art, the **Hamburger Bahnhof** and **Martin-Gropius-Bau** both host important temporary exhibitions. The **c/o** gallery**,** near Zoo station, is good for photography exhibitions.

Museum Berggruen

Schlossstrasse 1, Charlottenburg
www.smb.museum

A former private collection of works by Klee, Picasso, Matisse, Giacometti and others, located in an elegant Charlottenburg villa. It is across the street from the late seventeenth-century **Schloss Charlottenburg** with its opulent interiors.

Jewish Museum

Lindenstrasse 9–14, Kreuzberg
www.jmberlin.de

Daniel Libeskind's sheer metallic building is in the shape of a broken Star of David. It has a number of spaces that play with visitors' perspective, the Holocaust Tower and Garden of Exile.

Topography of Terror

Niederkirchnerstrasse 8, Kreuzberg
www.topographie.de

In the location of the headquarters of the SS and Gestapo, this museum about Nazi terror is a short walk from the former Nazi Air Force Ministry (now Ministry of Finance), the location of **Hitler's Bunker** and the Federal **Memorial to the Murdered Jews of Europe** (across the street are related memorials to murdered Sinti and Roma and persecuted homosexuals).

Berlin Wall Memorial

Bernauer Strasse 111, Wedding/Mitte
www.berliner-mauer-gedenkstaette.de

This large outdoor site along Bernauer Strasse includes reserved remnants of the Berlin Wall, an informative visitor centre and a viewing platform to the memorial of the former death strip below. A related site of remembrance is the **East Side Gallery** with its Berlin Wall murals and the **Berlin-Hohenschönhausen Memorial** at the site of a former Stasi prison. One of the best museums on the city's division is dedicated to everyday border experiences, in the small **Tränenpalast** (Palace of Tears) at Friedrichstrasse station.

Soviet War Memorial, Treptower Park

Puschkinallee, Treptow

Located just south of Kreuzberg, this Second World War memorial is the largest of its kind outside of Russia. It is a remarkable space, with an enormous Soviet soldier stepping on a swastika. A related site is the Stalinist avenue of **Karl-Marx-Allee** that stretches from Alexanderplatz and its **Television Tower** ('the Needle', with a great view from the top).

Further Afield

Potsdam, a city of approximately 150,000 on the southwest edge of Berlin is reachable in a little over half an hour from central Berlin by S-Bahn. Potsdam was favoured by the Prussian kings and is adorned with many palaces, including the **Schloss Sanssouci** (1747), with its terraced vineyard over the beautiful palace gardens.

On the Berlin side of the city limits are a number of beautiful lakes along the S-Bahn line, with summer swimming and beer gardens, including **Schlachtensee** and **Wannsee**, location of the **House of the Wannsee Conference** and the **Liebermann-Villa**. The western boundary of Berlin also corresponds to the well-maintained **Mauerweg** (Berlin Wall) **Bike Path** that continues 160 km passing through the centre of the city.

ENTERTAINMENT SITES

The Berlin Philharmonic
Herbert-von-Karajan-Strasse 1, Tiergarten
www.berliner-philharmoniker.de

Europe's most famous philharmonic orchestra plays in the 1963 yellow hall, part of the Kulturforum, near Potsdamer Platz, noted for its excellent acoustics. There are a number of other excellent orchestras in the city, including the **Deutsches Symphonie-Orchester** and the orchestra of the **Staatsoper**.

Schaubühne
Kurfürstendamm 153, Wilmersdorf
www.schaubühne.de

Berlin's most famously innovative theatre in the former West, directed by Thomas Ostermeier. They have selected performances with surtitles in English.

Berliner Ensemble
Bertolt-Brecht-Platz 1, Mitte
www.berliner-ensemble.de

This is Bertolt Brecht's old theatre. Other major theatres in Berlin are the Volksbühne, Deutsches Theater, Hebbel-am-Ufer and Maxim Gorki Theater (the latter two, which focus on experimental or immigrant theatre, surtitle almost all of their performances).

Staatsoper Unter den Linden

Unter den Linden 7, Mitte
www.staatsoper-berlin.de

The old State Opera House on Unter den Linden (temporarily in the Schiller Theater: Bismarckstrasse 110 until Autumn 2017) is under the direction of Daniel Barenboim (whose Barenboim-Said music academy opened its doors in Berlin in 2016). Other opera companies are the Komische Oper, the Deutsche Oper and the *Kiez*-oriented Neuköllner Oper.

Friedrichstadt-Palast

Friedrichstrasse 107, Mitte
www.palast.berlin

Sure to satisfy those with fine taste in kitsch, this cavernous East German theatre built in the 1980s in 'Kazakh railroad' style (see it to believe it) hosts revue shows. Think Las Vegas-meets-post-Communism, if you can.

Radialsystem

Holzmarktstrasse 33, Friedrichshain
www.radialsystem.de

A contemporary venue for dance and music along the river.

Berlin Film Festival

www.berlinale.de

Every February, one of Europe's most important film festivals, the '**Berlinale**', occurs in the city. It is also a festival where the general public can obtain tickets fairly easily. Most performances are located around Potsdamer Platz.

Kino International

Karl-Marx-Allee 33, Mitte
www.kino-international.com

During the year, it is highly recommended to catch a film at this theatre in the Socialist Realist style on Karl-Marx-Allee. Other good places to see films are the **Arsenal Kino** in the Filmmuseum in Potsdamer Platz and the cinemas in Hackescher Markt. In summer, many venues offer 'Sommerkino', or open-air cinema. 'OmU' means 'Original with Subtitles'.

Tempelhof Airfield

Tempelhofer Damm 90, Tempelhof
www.thf-berlin.de

Decommissioned in 2008, Tempelhof Airport is now a massive park where you can, remarkably, rollerblade and ride bikes down the runways. In the summer, it is the location for a number of festivals and public events. Much of the old airport infrastructure, including the 1920s terminal, remains (and, in 2017, houses approximately 1,300 refugees), as well as Cold War American military installations. The airfield is located south of Kreuzberg near Boddinstrasse U-8 or Platz der Luftbrücke U-6 stations.

Künstlerhaus Bethanien

Kottbusser Strasse 10, Kreuzberg
www.bethanien.de

Those interested in seeing studio spaces and the production of visual arts in Europe's arts capital may be disappointed outside of **Berlin Art Week** (usually in September), as most happens behind closed doors, and the work is sold elsewhere. That said, this international cultural centre in Kreuzberg, housed in a former hospital, offers opportunities to see artists working and attend openings.

HOTELS

Das Stue

Drakestrasse 1, Tiergarten
www.das-stue.com

Located in the former Danish Embassy, an elegant but quiet 1930s building retired alongside the Tiergarten. The name ('living room' in Danish) is something of an understatement: comfy high-end diplomatic elegance, with prices to match. A touch of old-world intrigue and a hotel one expects to see in the next Bond film.

Hotel Adlon Kempinski

Unter den Linden 77, Mitte
www.kempinski.com/adlon

Berlin's most famous hotel address: where presidents and the queen stay, with a view over the Brandenburg Gate. Known for its personal butler service. The Lorenz Adlon Esszimmer restaurant has two Michelin stars.

Hotel Oderberger

Oderberger Strasse 57–59, Prenzlauer Berg
www.hotel-oderberger.berlin

Located in what was a 1902 swimming pool, this new hotel has impressive vaulted public spaces and rooms overlooking a charming leafy street.

Michelberger Hotel

Warschauer Strasse 39, Friedrichshain
www.michelbergerhotel.com

A hip urban hotel for the club set, with a contemporary industrial aesthetic. It is steps away from the heart of Friedrichshain's nightlife.

The Circus

Weinbergsweg 1A, Mitte
www.circus-berlin.de

Excellent value in Mitte, the Circus has a hotel, a hostel and apartments. This highly rated hotel is known for being hip and friendly.

SPECIALITY SHOPPING

KaDeWe

Tauentzienstrasse 21–24, Charlottenburg
www.kadewe.de

The Kaufhaus des Westens is the largest department store in Continental Europe, and it has been around since 1907. The food floors at the top are Berlin favourites, especially the wine section. For Francophiles, Berlin has its own **Galeries Lafayette** in Mitte.

Voo
Oranienstrasse 24, Kreuzberg
www.vooberlin.com

Hipster emporium in Kreuzberg for men and women. Also has coffee and lifestyle books.

Fein und Ripp
Kastanienallee 91/92, Prenzlauer Berg
www.feinundripp.de

A shop that sells men's clothes from the 1920s and '30s, and other eras. Think baggy trousers with braces.

Trippen
Rosenthaler Strasse 40–41, Mitte
en.trippen.com

Beautifully designed and comfortable shoes made in the Berlin area. Several showrooms in the city, including this one in the Hackesche Höfe.

Hard Wax
Paul-Lincke-Ufer 44A, Kreuzberg
www.hardwax.com

Perhaps Berlin's most famous record store, focusing on electronic music.

Modulor
Prinzenstrasse 85, Kreuzberg
www.modulor.de

Enormous multi-level stationery and office supply store at Moritzplatz, very dangerous for graphophiles.

Winterfeldt Schokoladen
Goltzstrasse 23, Schöneberg
www.winterfeldt-schokoladen.de

Large variety of international chocolates for sale in an intimate atmosphere. You may also enjoy the small hot chocolate café.

Markthalle 9
Eisenbahnstrasse 42–43, Kreuzberg
markthalleneun.de

Artisanal market hall in Kreuzberg, and centre of the foodie revolution in the city: Thursday nights (street food), Tues/Fri/Sat daytime market. The very popular breakfast market is held monthly. Inside for food every day of the week except Sunday is the **Kantine** (local and organic), **Sironi** bakery, **Mani in Pasta** (fresh pasta and lunch dishes), **Big Stuff** barbeque meats (brisket, pork belly and so on), **Kumpel & Kuele** butchers (which seems to be run by electronic music DJs) and **Café 9** (coffee).

Turkish Market
Maybachufer, Neukölln
www.tuerkenmarkt.de

On Tuesday and Fridays, this sprawling mostly food market stretches along the Maybachufer in Kreuzberg. A central meeting point of the Turkish community.

Treptow Flea Market
Eichenstrasse 4, Treptow
www.hallentrödelmarkt-berlin-treptow.de

Open Saturday and Sundays, this flea market sells everything from vintage furniture to old door handles, to bicycles. Another celebrated weekend flea market is at **Ostbahnhof.**

RESTAURANTS

Reinstoff
Schlegelstrasse 26C, Mitte
www.reinstoff.eu

Two-star Michelin that specializes in Nordic-style molecular cooking.

Lokal
Linienstrasse 160, Mitte
www.lokal-berlin.blogspot.de

Contemporary, regional food. Hip.

Café Einstein Stammhaus
Kurfürstenstrasse 58, Schöneberg
www.cafeeinstein.com

Old-world and iconic Mitteleuropa coffee house on Kürfurstenstrasse.

Nobelhart & Schmutzig
Friedrichstrasse 218, Kreuzberg
www.nobelhartundschmutzig.com

Regional cuisine, local ingredients, Nordic touches.

Lamazère
Stuttgarter Platz 18, Charlottenburg
www.lamazere.de

Michelin-rated classic French bistro. A culinary embassy of sorts for French expats in Berlin.

Renger Patzsch
Wartburgstrasse 54, Schöneberg
www.renger-patzsch.com

French–German fusion, neighbourhood restaurant, also with a vegetarian set menu. Smart/elegant.

Tulus Lotrek
Fichtestraße 24, Kreuzberg
www.tuluslotrek.de

The restaurant's name puns on that of the French post-Impressionist painter – the idea is that their interpretations of French classics are anything but conventional. Look out for the owner, whose dress, at times, matches the floral wallpaper exactly.

Bieberbau
Durlacher Strasse 15, Schöneberg
www.bieberbau-berlin.de

Set in a quiet residential street, in a late 19th-century plasterer's studio, Bieberbau is a one-star Michelin restaurant focusing on regional cuisine. Think creative combinations such as poppy seed, carrot and cod, or cherry, walnut and watercress. It also offers a vegetarian set menu.

Gasthaus Figl
Urbanstrasse 47, Kreuzberg
www.gasthaus-figl.de

German Flammkuchen and daily specials.

Sarods
Friesenstrasse 22, Kreuzberg
www.sarods.de

Thai, casual, very good ingredients, with vegetarian options.

STREET FOOD AND *STUBEN* (PUBS)

Dicke Wirten
Carmerstrasse 9, Charlottenburg
www.dicke-wirtin.de

Ancient Berlin pub and grub.

Adana Grillhaus
Manteuffelstrasse 86, Kreuzberg
www.adanagrillhaus.de

Lamb chops and Turkish grill.

Imbiss 204
Prenzlauer Allee 204, Prenzlauer Berg
www.imbiss204.de

Gastronomic versions of Berlin classics but at an Imbiss, huge portions.

Prater Biergarten
Kastanienallee 7–9, Prenzlauer Berg
www.pratergarten.de

Classic outdoor beer garden, with sit-down inside restaurant.

Azzam
Sonnenallee 54, Neukölln

Falafel take-away (Palestinian).

Wittys
Wittenbergplatz 5, Charlottenburg
www.wittys-berlin.de

Berlin's best currywurst and chips, and it is organic. Compare with the more famous **Curry 36**, which also has chains throughout the city.

Imren
Boppstrasse 4, Kreuzberg
www.imren-grill.de

Known for the best doner kebab in Berlin. Apparently the meat is so tender because it is marinated in milk.

Burgermeister
Oberbaumstrasse 8, Kreuzberg
www.burgermeister.berlin

Hamburgers under the U-Bahn Line, and also now at Kottbusser Tor.

Mister Minsch
Yorckstrasse 15, Kreuzberg
www.mr-minsch-torten.de

Wonderful cakes. I especially like their double chocolate cake and their rhubarb crumble (*Streusel*) cake. The cheesecakes are exquisite, especially with sour cherries.

Stadtklause
Bernburger Strasse 35, Kreuzberg
www.stadtklause.de

Berlin lunch specialities served cafeteria-style in a creaky historic house.

BARS AND CLUBS

mostly queer/gay marked with *

Not Only Riesling

Schleiermacherstrasse 25, Charlottenburg
www.not-only-riesling.de

German white wine specialist, bar and shop. Second location in Kreuzberg.

Villa Neukölln

Hermannstrasse 233, Neukölln
www.villaneukoelln.de

Hipster-central, in a gentrifying *Kiez*. Thursday 'On With the Show' parties with 1920s swing music and dancing.

Roses*

Oranienstrasse 187, Kreuzberg

In Kreuzberg's 'alternative' gay scene, decadent grungy gay bar with pink faux-fur walls. Like being inside a Muppet. Cross-reference with the smoky and crowded **Möbel Olfe*** nearby, or the Queer community centre with pub quiz at **Südblock***. Next door to Roses, at the **SO36** club, look out for the gay Middle Eastern night monthly called '**GayHane**'*, or gay bingo run by drag queens.

Panorama Bar

Am Wriezener Bahnhof, Friedrichshain
www.berghain.de

Infamous electronic music club space in a Communist power plant. **Berghain*** on Saturday nights, when several rooms are open, has an infamous door policy. Don't ask what happens in the basement.

://about blank

Markgrafendamm 24c, Friedrichshain
www.aboutparty.net

Relatively low-attitude nightclub set in a formerly illegal industrial space. They have a great garden in the summer and host the monthly alternative gay party **ButtOns***.

RAW-Gelände

Revaler Strasse, Friedrichshain

In the industrial yards west of Revaler Strasse are a great number of club and bar spaces, including **Haubentaucher** (the area's gentrifier, with swimming pool) and **Cassiopeia**. At the time of writing, this space was coming under pressure from local authorities and investors.

Club der Visionäre

Am Flutgraben 1, Treptow
www.clubdervisionaere.com

Along the canal: fabulous outdoor electronic music lounge.

Strandbars

Along the Spree, Friedrichshain

Outdoor beach bars with electronic music, along the river bank in summer near Ostbahnhof. Many are closing as the area is exploited by developers. Try Holzmarkt or Kater Blau, both on Holzmarktstrasse.

Clärchens Ballhaus

Auguststrasse 24, Mitte
www.ballhaus.de

This dance hall and restaurant, which opened in 1913, is located in a half-bombarded building. It oozes charm. Some nights waltz, others cha-cha, others with live band or orchestra. Upstairs is an old-world hall of mirrors with candlelit dinners.

Kosmetiksalon Babette

Karl-Marx-Allee 36, Mitte
www.barbabette.com

Soviet modernist pavilion, and cocktails, on Karl-Marx-Allee across from Kino International.

Chronology

1183 CE
First evidence of settlement in Berlin

1237
Cölln first mentioned in writing

1244
Berlin first mentioned in writing

1307
Cölln joins Berlin administratively

1415
House of Hohenzollern acquire Brandenburg

1539
Protestant Reformation

1618–48
Thirty Years War

1640
Friedrich Wilhelm (the Great Elector) reigns

1671
Arrival of Jewish families from Vienna

1685
Edict of Tolerance, followed by French immigration

1688
Friedrich III reigns

1701
Kingdom of Prussia, Friedrich III is crowned Friedrich I

1713
Friedrich Wilhelm I (the Soldier King) reigns

1734
New Customs Wall

1740
Friedrich II (the Great) reigns

1743
Moses Mendelssohn arrives in Berlin

1786
Friedrich Wilhelm II (the much-beloved) reigns

1791
Building of the Brandenburg Gate

1797
Friedrich Wilhelm III reigns

1806
Napoleon's troops arrive in Berlin

1813
Battle of Nations (French defeat)

1840
Friedrich Wilhelm IV reigns

1848
Revolution in Berlin defeated

1861
Wilhelm I reigns

1862
Holbrecht Plan

1871
Germany unified as an empire

1888
Wilhelm II rules as Kaiser

1914–18
First World War

1918
Abdication of Wilhelm II, republic declared

1919
Defeat of Spartacus Uprising, Versailles Treaty

1920
Berlin City Law

1923
Hyperinflation

1929
Stock market crash

1933
National Socialists assume power

1935
Nuremberg Laws

1936
Berlin Olympics

1938
Night of Broken Glass (*Kristallnacht*)

1939–45
Second World War

1942
Wannsee Conference

1945
Hitler's suicide, Berlin's capitulation to Red Army, 'Zero hour'

1947–9
Berlin Blockade and Air Lift

1949
Declaration of two Germanies: East and West

1953
Soviet troops put down workers' uprising in East

1961
Guestworker Treaty between Turkey and West Germany

1961
Berlin Wall is built

1989
Berlin Wall falls

1990
German Reunification

References

All translations are mine unless otherwise noted.

p. 27 'The apparent mismatch between the force wielded by the Prussian state and the domestic resources available to sustain it helps to explain one of the most curious features of Prussia's history as a European power, namely the alternation of moments of precocious strength with moments of perilous weakness.' Christopher Clark, *Iron Kingdom* (London, 2006), p. xxv.

p. 29 Thomas Carlyle, *History of Friedrich II of Prussia*, vol. III (Leipzig, 1858), ch. 10.

p. 34 Martin Düspohl, *Kleine Kreuzberger Geschichte* (Berlin, 2012), p. 13.

p. 37 Marlies K. Danziger, ed., *James Boswell: The Journal of His German and Swiss Travels, 1764* (Edinburgh, 2008).

p. 40 Clark, *Iron Kingdom*, p. 82.

p. 41 Ibid., pp. 101–11.

pp. 41–2 Johann Kaspar Riesbeck, *Travels Through Germany, in a Series of Letters*, vol. II, trans. Paul Henry Maty (Vienna, 1787), p. 245.

p. 42 Clark, *Iron Kingdom,* p. 187.

p. 42 Immanuel Kant, 'What is Enlightenment?', 1784.

p. 43 Otto Bardong, ed., *Friedrich der Grosse* (Darmstadt, 1982), p. 542. Also quoted in Clark, *Iron Kingdom,* p. 253.

p. 43 Amos Elon, *The Pity of it All: A Portrait of the German-Jewish Epoch, 1743–1933* (New York, 2002), p. 4.

p. 44 Ismar Elbogen, J. Guttmann and E. Mittwoch, eds, *Moses Mendelssohn, Gesammelte Schriften, Jubiläumsausgabe*, trans. Richard Levy Moses (Berlin, 1930), pp. 7–17.

p. 44 'Jeder soll nach seiner Façon selig werden', from the king's papers; a facsimile can be found in Georg Büchmann, *Geflügelte Worte* (Berlin, 2007).

p. 44 Clark, *Iron Kingdom*, p. 185.

p. 47 David E. Cartwright, *Schopenhauer: A Biography* (Cambridge, 2010), pp. 156–7.

p. 47 Ibid., p. 484.

p. 47 Ibid., pp. 364–7.

p. 49 Sebastian Hensel, Mendelssohn's nephew, quoted in R. Larry Todd, ed., *Mendelssohn Essays* (London, 2013), p. 41.

p. 50 A.J.P. Taylor, *The Course of German History* (London, 1961), p. 69.

p. 51 Quoted in David Blackbourn, *Fontana History of Germany, 1780–1918* (London, 1997), p. xiii.

p. 53 Mark Twain, 'The Chicago of Europe', *Chicago Daily Tribune* (3 April 1892).

p. 53 David Clay Large, *Berlin* (New York, 2000), p. 9.

p. 53 Ibid.

p. 56 Theodor Fontane, *Effi Briest*, trans. Hugh Rorrison and Helen Chambers (London, 1995), p. 143.

p. 57 Moritz Gottlieb Saphir, *Conversations-Lexikon für Geist, Witz und Humor*, vol. 1 (Dresden, 1852), p. 96.

p. 58 Large, *Berlin*, p. 18.

p. 58 Twain, 'The Chicago of Europe'.

p. 59 Willy Rosen, *Das ist Berlin auf der Tauentzien* (Berlin, 1925).

p. 59 Fritz Stern, *Einstein's German World* (Princeton, NJ, 1999).

p. 62 *Max Liebermann: From Realism to Impressionism*, exh. cat., Jewish Museum, New York, 10 March–30 July 2006 (New York, 2005).

p. 63 Large, *Berlin*, p. 8.

p. 64 The Annie Oakley anecdote is the subject of much debate. See David Clay Large, 'Thanks, But No Cigar', in *What If? The World's Foremost Military Historians Imagine What Might Have Been* (New York, 1999), pp. 290–91.

p. 66 Hans Fallada, *Iron Gustav: A Berlin Family Chronicle* [1938], trans. Philip Owens (London, 2014), p. 334.

p. 67 'Der Geist von Berlin', *Schwäbischer Merkur*, no. 14, 10 January 1919.

p. 69 *Gershom Scholem: A Life in Letters, 1914–1982*, ed. and trans. Anthony David Skinner (Cambridge, MA, 2002), pp. 125–7.

p. 69 Stefan Zweig, *Die Welt von Gestern* (Stockholm, 1942), ch. 13.

p. 70 Franz Hessel, 'Der Verdächtige', in *Spazieren in Berlin* [1929] (Berlin, 2011), p. 23.

p. 72 Quoted in Alex Ross, *The Rest is Noise* (London, 2007), p. 218.

p. 73 Christopher Isherwood, *Goodbye to Berlin* [1939] (New York, 2011), p. 24.

p. 73 Bundesarchiv, Bild 102-12334/CC-BY-SA. French Premier Pierre Laval and Foreign Minister Aristide Briand at the Adlon, 1 September 1931.

p. 74 Irmgard Keun, *The Artificial Silk Girl* [1932], trans. Kathie von Ankum (New York, 2002).

p. 74 Isherwood, *Goodbye to Berlin*, p. 159.

p. 75 Ibid., p. 181.

p. 77 The debates surrounding the playbook of the Reichstag fire are extensive. For a summary see Richard Evans's review (of Benjamin Carter Hett, *Burning the Reichstag: An Investigation into the Third Reich's Enduring Mystery* (Oxford, 2014)), 'The Conspiracists', *London Review of Books*, XXXVI/9 (8 May 2014), pp. 3–9.

p. 77 Rudolf Diels, *Lucifer ante portas: . . . es spricht der erste Chef der Gestapo* (Zurich, 1949), pp. 142–4. English translation from Jeremy Noakes and Geoffrey Pridham, eds, *Nazism, 1919–1945* (Exeter, 1998), vol. I, pp. 139–41.

p. 79 Quoted in Large, *Berlin*, p. 259.

p. 79 Alexandra Ritchie, *Faust's Metropolis* (London, 1999), p. 416; Large, *Berlin*, p. 263.

p. 80 Hermann Rügler, 'Was der Berliner von der Geschichte seiner Stadt wissen Muss', *Sonderheft Berliner Illustrirte Zeitung* (Berlin, 1937), p. 13. Also quoted in Ritchie, *Faust's Metropolis*, p. 408.

p. 81 There is debate on the source of the marble in Mohrenstrasse station. My summary of the debate you can read online: Joseph Pearson, 'Hitler's Bloody Palace: Mohrenstrasse', The Needle, www.needleberlin.com, 17 July 2011.

p. 82 Richard Evans, *The Coming of the Third Reich* (London, 2004), p. 412.

p. 82 Ibid., p. 418.

p. 83 Peter Gay, *My German Question* (New Haven, CT, 1998), p. 134.

p. 83 Ritchie, *Faust's Metropolis*, p. 436.

p. 86 See Susan Sontag, 'Fascinating Fascism', *New York Review of Books* (6 February 1975).

p. 86 An 'incalculable loss Germans inflicted, as it were, on themselves after 1933'. Elon, *The Pity of it All*, p. 10.

p. 87 William Shirer, *Berlin Diary: The Journal of a Foreign Correspondent, 1934–1941* (New York, 1941), 3 September 1939.

p. 87 Ibid., 18 July 1940.

p. 88 Ibid., 15 October 1940.

p. 89 *Frankfurter Zeitung* (20 February 1943), p. 7. Reprinted in Helmut Heiber, ed., *Goebbels Reden 1932–1945* (Bindlach, 1991), pp. 203–5. English translation from Joachim Remak, ed., *The Nazi Years: A Documentary History* (Englewood Cliffs, NJ, 1969), pp. 91–2.

p. 90 Inge Deutschkron, *Outcast: A Jewish Girl in Wartime Berlin*. Also quoted in Marion A. Kaplan, *Between Dignity and Despair: Jewish Life in Nazi Germany* (Oxford, 1999), p. 158.

p. 93 Anonymous [Martha Hillers], *A Woman in Berlin*, trans. Philip Boehm (London, 2004), p. 83.

p. 94 Antony Beevor, *The Fall of Berlin* (New York, 2002), p. 2.

p. 95 For further reading on Berlin in 1945, see Ian Kershaw, *The End: Germany, 1944–5* (London, 2012).

p. 98 Timothy Vogt, *Denazification in Soviet-occupied Germany: Brandenburg 1945–1948* (Cambridge, MA, 2000).

p. 99 Ibid.

p. 99 See the exhibition rooms of the Märkisches Museum for useful documents and photographs on this period.

p. 100 Marie Todeskino, 'The Hero of the Berlin Airlift', *Deutsche Welle*, www.dw.com, 18 July 2013.

p. 100 David Lauterborn, 'Interview with Gail Halvorsen, the Berlin Candy Bomber', www.historynet.com, 29 April 2009.

p. 102 Rita Chin, *The Guestworker Question in Postwar Germany* (Cambridge, 2009), p. 39.

p. 102 Kerstin Schilling, 'Die Generation West-Berlin und die Freiheit', in *War jewesen: West Berlin 1961–1989* (Berlin, 2009), pp. 188–9.

p. 104 Quoted in the BBC documentary *In Love with Terror* (2002).

p. 104 *Der Abend, Eine Zeitung für Berlin*, quoted in Bommi Baumann, *Wie alles anfing* (Berlin, 1994), p. 58.

p. 104 Ingeborg Bachmann, 'Ein Ort Fuer Zurfaelle' [1965] (1999), in *War jewesen: West Berlin 1961–1989* (Berlin, 2009), p. 41.

p. 104 *Wir Kinder von Bahnhof Zoo* (1978).

p. 105 '*Uncut* Interviews David Bowie on Berlin (1999)', www.davidbowie.com, accessed 27 October 2016.

p. 108 The project website is 'Automate Virtual Reconstruction of Ripped Stasi Files', www.ipk.fraunhofer.de.

p. 108 Laura Poitras is based in Berlin, where her film *CITIZENFOUR* on Edward Snowden was produced. The German Greens, with strong public support, have been very active in lobbying for Germany to provide Snowden with asylum.

p. 111 A good discussion of this argument can be found in Brian Ladd, *Ghosts of Berlin: Confronting German History in the Urban Landscape* (Chicago, IL, 1997), p. 29, where he quotes East German writer Lutz Rathenow, *Ost-Berlin: Leben vor dem Mauerfall* (Berlin, 2005).

p. 112 Sebastian Heiduschke, *East German Cinema: DEFA and Film History* (London, 2013), p. 103.

p. 133 Director Armin Petras quoted in Joseph Pearson, 'An Autopsy of the GDR: Armin Petras' Divided Heaven', *Pearson's Preview*, www.schaubuehne.de, 28 December 2014.

p. 118 Cordt Schnibben, 'The Guard who Opened the Berlin Wall', www.spiegel.de, 9 November 2009.

p. 125 Matthias Bernnt, Britta Grell and Andrej Holm, eds, *The Berlin Reader* (Bielefeld, 2013), p. 23.

p. 125 Joanna McKay, 'Berlin-Brandenburg? Nein danke! The Referendum on the Proposed *Länderfusion*', *German Politics*, v/3 (1996), pp. 485–502.

p. 125 See the data of the Berlin Institute for Population and Development: www.berlin-institut.org.

p. 126 Bernnt, Grell and Holm, eds, *The Berlin Reader* (Bielefeld, 2013), p. 15.

p. 126 See statistical agency of Berlin-Brandenburg: www.statistik-berlin-brandenburg.de.

p. 126 From the graphic novel of the same name: OL, *Die Mütter vom Kollwitzplatz* (Oldenburg, 2013).

p. 126 Jody K. Biehl, 'Germany's Baby Bust: Why aren't Germans Having Babies?', *Spiegel Online*, www.spiegel.de, 14 January 2005.

p. 126 Nirmala Rao, *Cities in Transition: Growth, Change and Governance in Six Metropolitan Areas* (London, 2008), pp. 97–8.

p. 127 Alexander Neubacher and Michael Sauga, 'Germany's Disappointing Reunification', www.spiegel.de, 1 July 2010.

p. 129 Gabriela Walde, 'Starfotograf Wolfgang Tillmans zieht von London nach Berlin', *Berliner Morgenpost* (13 January 2014).

p. 129 'Ten Questions for Wolfgang Tillmans', *Phaidon*, uk.phaidon.com, accessed 27 October 2015.

p. 133 Ben Knight, 'Berlin Sued over Dangerous Conditions for Refugees', *Deutsche Welle*, www.dw.com, 8 December 2015.

p. 133 Bernnt, Grell and Holm, eds, *The Berlin Reader*, p. 16.

p. 139 For statistics on trees on Berlin city streets, see 'Stadtbäume, Daten und Fakten', www.stadtentwicklung.berlin.de.

p. 139 Frank O'Hara, 'Meditations in an Emergency', 1954.

p. 148 A 2013 exhibition, *Zehlendorf wurde braun*, explored the popularity of the neighbourhood with Nazi elites. See 'Zehlendorf wurde Braun: Täter und Opfer Lebten Tür an Tür', *Berliner Zeitung* (1 October 2013).

p. 149 'Riesenwels beisst Schwimmerin', *Die Welt* (3 June 2008).

p. 150 Hans Fallada, *Alone in Berlin* [1947], trans. Michael Hofmann (London, 2009), p. 301.

p. 150 These reflections on this photograph can also be found on my blog: Joseph Pearson, 'Schlachtensee 1940', The Needle, www.needleberlin.com, 4 May 2010.

p. 151 See statistical information of the Land of Berlin, available online at www.statistik-berlin-brandenburg.de.

p. 157 John Green, 'Heinz Berggruen: Obituary', *The Guardian* (23 May 2007).

p. 157 See Devin Leonard, 'Deep Thoughts with the Homeless Billionaire', *Bloomberg*, www.bloomberg.com, 27 September 2012.

p. 158 Large, *Berlin*, p. 58.

p. 162 Markus Sebastian Braun, ed., *Berlin: The Architecture Guide* (Salenstein, 2012).

p. 165 See the architect's website for detailed information and images about the Neues Museum project: www.davidchipperfield.co.uk.

p. 175 'Degussa to Continue Work on Holocaust Memorial', *Deutsche Welle*, www.dw.com, 14 November 2003.

p. 180 Statistical information on Berlin's Jewish population is gleaned from a number of sources: Donald Snyder, 'Jews Stream Back to Germany', *Forward* (8 April 2012); *Jerusalem Post*, 'Gesellschaft: Berlin-hype in Israel', *Deutsche Welle*, www.dw.com, 31 October 2013; Peter Münch, 'Berlin, wir fahren nach Berlin', *Süddeutsche Zeitung* (13 October 2013); Gisela Dachs, 'Berlin, Diaspora der Israelis', *Die Zeit* (28 October 2013). Numbers from the Jüdische Gemeinde can be found online at www.jg-berlin.org/institutionen/integration.html, accessed 27 October 2016.

p. 180 These reflections on this evening can also be found on my blog: Joseph Pearson, 'Berlin's Gay-friendly Shabbat . . . featuring an appearance by the Police, and a reflection on the lessons of Secularism', The Needle, www.needleberlin.com, 19 January 2015.

p. 183 Philip Oltermann, 'From Grotesque to Quirky: A History of Berlin Told through U-Bahn Typography', *The Guardian* (11 March 2015).

p. 183 Mathias Hiller, 'Frakturschriften bei der Berliner S-Bahn', *Signal*, IX–X (January 1996), pp. 15–16.

p. 187 Christopher Isherwood, 'Berlin Diary, Autumn 1930', in *Goodbye to Berlin*, pp. 3–4.

p. 187 Christopher Isherwood, *Christopher and his Kind* [1976] (London, 2012), p. 3.

p. 190 Robert Beachy, *Gay Berlin: Birthplace of a Modern Identity* (New York, 2014).

p. 193 Joseph Pearson, 'Goodbye to Berlin? La JohnJoseph's "Trial Separation" and his New Novel', The Needle, www.needleberlin.com, 29 September 2014.

p. 194 FKK has come to be a byword for 'a brothel' for many visiting foreigners, but, especially in former East Germany, it is simply a phrase that means nudism.

p. 196 See 'Berlins Neues Kreuzberg Zentrum', www.failedarchitecture.com, accessed 30 August 2016.

p. 202 Katharina Wagner, 'Mobilmachung im Neuköllner Schillerkiez', *tip-Berlin* (30 August 2011).

p. 202 See the documentary film *Welcome Goodbye*, dir. Nana T. Rebhan (2014).

p. 202 Ann-Kathrin Nezik, 'Tourism Troubles: Berlin Cracks Down on Vacation Rentals', *Spiegel Online*, www.spiegel.de, 10 April 2015. Julian Trauthig, 'Die Mietpreisbremse scheint zu wirken', *Frankfurter Allgemeine Zeitung* (8 July 2015).

p. 207 Every couple of years there is a new spate of such articles, in the spirit of a high school popularity contest, about how 'cool' Berlin is. I set this chapter in the summer, but some most recent examples are from winter 2014: Zeke Turner, 'Brooklyn on the Spree: Brooklyn Bohemians Invade Berlin's Techno Scene', *New York Times* (21 February 2014); Max Read, 'Berlin is Over. What's Next?', *Gawker* (24 February 2014); Thomas Rogers, 'Berghain: The Secretive, Sex-fueled World of Techno's Coolest Club', *Rolling Stone* (6 February 2014); Verena Mayer, 'Tourismus in der Hauptstadt: "Berlin is Over"', *Süddeutsche Zeitung* (6 March 2014); Thomas Loy, 'Ende eines Trends?: Berlin ist nicht mehr die coolste Stadt der Welt', *Der Tagesspiele* (6 March 2014).

Suggested Reading and Viewing

Books about Berlin, available in English

Adam, Hans-Christian, *Berlin: Portrait of a City* (Cologne, 2007)
Anonymous, *A Woman in Berlin* [1954], trans. Philip Boehm (London, 2004)
Beachy, Robert, *Gay Berlin: Birthplace of a Modern Identity* (New York, 2014)
Bernt, Matthias, Britta Grell and Andrej Holm, eds, *The Berlin Reader* (Bielefeld, 2013)
Braun, Markus Sebastian, ed., *Berlin: The Architecture Guide* (Salenstein, 2012)
Clay Large, David, *Berlin* (New York, 2000)
Darnton, Robert, *Berlin Journal, 1989–1990* (New York, 1991)
Deutschkron, Inge, *Outcast: A Jewish Girl in Wartime Berlin* (New York, 1990)
Döblin, Alfred, *Berlin Alexanderplatz* [1929], trans. Eugene Jolas (London, 2004)
Elon, Amos, *The Pity of it All: A Portrait of the German-Jewish Epoch, 1743–1933* (New York, 2002)
Fallada, Hans, *Alone in Berlin* [1947], trans. Michael Hofmann (London, 2009)
——, *Iron Gustav: A Berlin Family Chronicle* [1937], trans. Philip Owens (London, 2014)
Fontane, Theodor, *Effi Briest* [1895], trans. Hugh Rorrison (London, 2001)
Funder, Anna, *Stasiland* (London, 2003)
Gay, Peter, *My German Question: Growing Up in Nazi Berlin* (New Haven, CT, 1998)
Haffner, Ernst, *Blood Brothers*, trans. Michael Hofmann (New York, 2015)

Isherwood, Christopher, *Christopher and his Kind* [1976] (London, 2012)
——, *Goodbye to Berlin* [1939] (New York, 2012)
——, *Mr Norris Changes Trains* [1935] (London, 2005)
Jordan, Jennifer A., *Structures of Memory: Understanding Urban Change in Berlin and Beyond* (Palo Alto, CA, 2006)
Keun, Irmgard, *The Artificial Silk Girl* [1932], trans. Kathie von Ankum (New York, 2002)
Ladd, Brian, *Ghosts of Berlin: Confronting German History in the Urban Landscape* (Chicago, IL, 1997)
Larson, Erik, *In the Garden of Beasts* (New York, 2011)
Maclean, Rory, *Berlin: Imagine a City* (London, 2014)
Özdamar, Emile Sevgi, *The Bridge of the Golden Horn*, trans. Martin Chalmers (London, 2007)
Richie, Alexandra, *Faust's Metropolis* (London, 1999)
Ross, Alex, *The Rest is Noise* (New York, 2007)
Roth, Joseph, *What I Saw*, trans. Michael Hofmann (New York, 2003)
Schneider, Peter, *Berlin Now*, trans. Sophie Schlondorff (London, 2014)
——, *The Wall Jumper*, trans. Leigh Hafrey (Chicago, IL, 1989)
Shirer, William L., *Berlin Diary: The Journal of a Foreign Correspondent, 1934–1941* (New York, 1941)
Till, Karen E., *The New Berlin: Memory, Politics, Place* (Minneapolis, MN, 2005)
Tucholsky, Kurt, *Berlin! Berlin!*, trans. Cindy Opitz (Berlin, 2013)

Films

Aimée and Jaguar, dir. Max Färberböck (1999)
Berlin Calling, dir. Hannes Stöhr (2008)
Berlin is in Germany, dir. Hannes Stöhr (2001)
Berlin, Schönhauser Corner, dir. Gerhard Klein (1957)
Berlin: Symphony of a Great City, dir. Walter Ruttmann (1927)
The Bourne Supremacy, dir. Paul Greengrass (2004)
Cabaret, dir. Bob Fosse (1972)
Christiane F., dir. Uli Edel (1981)
Different from the Others, dir. Richard Oswald (1919)

The Divided Sky, dir. Konrad Wolf (1964)
Downfall, dir. Oliver Hirschbiegel (2004)
The Edukators, dir. Hans Weingartner (2004)
Emil and the Detectives, dir. Gerhard Lamprecht (1931)
A Foreign Affair, dir. Billy Wilder (1948)
Germany, Year Zero, dir. Roberto Rossellini (1948)
Ghosts, dir. Christian Petzold (2005)
Goodbye Lenin, dir. Wolfgang Becker (2003)
Harvest, dir. Benjamin Cantu (2011)
The Last Laugh, dir. F. W. Murnau (1924)
The Legend of Paul and Paula, dir. Heiner Carow (1973)
Life is All You Get, dir. Wolfgang Becker (1997)
The Life and Death of Colonel Blimp, dir. Michael Powell and Emeric Pressburger (1943)
The Lives of Others, dir. Florian Henckel von Donnersmarck (2006)
Lola and Billy the Kid, dir. Kutlug Ataman (1999)
M, dir. Fritz Lang (1931)
Metropolis, dir. Fritz Lang (1927)
Murderers Among Us, dir. Wolfgang Staudte (1948)
Neukölln Unlimited, dir. Agostino Imondi and Dietmar Ratsch (2010)
No Place to Go, dir. Oskar Roehler (2000)
Oh Boy! (*A Coffee in Berlin*), dir. Jan Ole Gerster (2012)
Olympia, dir. Leni Riefenstahl (1938)
One, Two, Three, dir. Billy Wilder (1961)
People on Sunday, dir. Curt and Robert Siodmak (1930)
Rabbit à la Berlin, dir. Bartosz Kanopka (2009)
Run Lola Run, dir. Tom Tykwer (1998)
Solo Sunny, dir. Konrad Wolf (1980)
Sonnenallee, dir. Leander Haussmann (1999)
Stroszek, dir. Werner Herzog (1977)
Three, dir. Tom Tykwer (2010)
Victoria, dir. Sebastian Schipper (2015)
Walk on Water, dir. Eytan Fox (2005)
Wings of Desire, dir. Wim Wenders (1987)

Acknowledgements

I would like to thank James Helgeson for being such a sharp and sensitive reader, and partner in discovering Berlin on both sunny and dark days. And I would not have discovered the best of the city without the help of my Berlin friends.

I am grateful to the historians William Mulligan, at University College Dublin, and Roland Pietsch, at New York University-Berlin, for their astute advice on the manuscript. All mistakes, omissions and the like, in the final version, are entirely my responsibility. I would also like to thank my students, who enrolled in 'Berlin History and Culture' at NYU-Berlin for their insights, and NYU-Berlin director Gabriella Etmektsoglou for helping me make Berlin my classroom. Many thanks to Brendan Simms for continued good conversation over the years.

I am indebted to my colleagues at the Schaubühne Theater for opening doors to Berlin's arty demi-monde: especially Maja Zade, Marius von Mayenburg, Thomas Ostermeier and the crew at the Press Department. Many thanks to Markus Hoffmann in New York for providing such valuable advice at the beginning of this project.

A special thanks to my editor Vivian Constantinopoulos in London for liking my blog, The Needle, and for asking me to write for Reaktion Books about Berlin.

Thanks finally to my family, especially my parents, who have been so supportive and loving.

Photo Acknowledgements

The author and the publishers wish to express their thanks to the below sources of illustrative material and/or permission to reproduce it.

© bpk-Bildagentur: p. 10; Bundesarchiv, Koblenz: pp. 84, 88; Courtesy of the Cambridge University Library, Map Room: p. 32 (Atlas.2.75.6), pp. 30–31, 33 top, 63, 141, 160 (Views.a.257.90.2); Arno Declair: p. 154; Amy Ewen: p. 16; Galerie Buchholz: pp. 128–9; GerardM: p. 8; James Helgeson: pp. 152–3; iStockphoto: pp. 6 (AndreaAstes), 7 (code6d), 9 top & bottom (lecatnoir), 11 top, 12–13 (cbies), (totalpics), 22 (ewg3D), 35 (MichaelUtech), 43 (AndreyKrav), 81 (lucamato), 103 (hsvrs), 112 (gameover2012), 136 (lechnatoir), 138 (fotoVoyager), 208–9 (lechatnoir), 212 (Rocky89); Landesarchiv Berlin: p. 74; Luukas: p. 40; © Estate of Will McBride: p. 147; Museum Blindenwerkstatt Otto Weidt in der Stiftung (MBOW): p. 90; Joseph Pearson: pp. 11 bottom, 14, 15, 26, 27, 28, 29, 33 bottom, 38, 46, 48, 55, 56, 72, 94, 96, 107, 109, 110, 113, 118, 119, 127, 131, 132, 140, 146, 149, 157, 158, 164, 166, 171, 172, 173, 174, 178–9, 183, 185, 188, 189, 193, 196, 197, 198, 200, 201, 202, 204, 206, 207, 210, 211; REX Shutterstock: pp. 92 (Gro), 120–21; Courtesy of Schaubühne Theatre: p. 114 (© Photo by Dorothea Tuch); Shutterstock: p. 10 (multitel); © Stiftung Stadtmuseum Berlin, Reproduktion: Oliver Ziebe, Berlin: p. 60; Courtesy Titanic magazine: p. 122.

Index

Page numbers in italics refer to illustrations